KV-192-346

# Contents

## Introduction

■ ■ ■

## Content Guidance

■ ■ ■

## Questions and Answers

# Introduction

## About this guide

This is a guide to Unit 1 of the new Edexcel AS psychology specification. Before looking at what this guide is all about, here is some good news. You can pass the exam for this unit and you can do well. How can I draw this conclusion without knowing you? Because you are reading this guide.

Students who take the trouble to read this sort of guide:
- are motivated to do well
- have an idea about where to look for help
- understand what unit they are taking and with which examination board/awarding body
- know something about active learning — we can learn better if we engage in tasks, such as using this sort of student guide

So you already have a lot of the skills and knowledge you need — hence my claim that you can do well.

However, this guide:
- is not a textbook — there is no substitute for reading the required material and taking notes
- does not tell you the actual questions on your paper or give you the answers

### Aims

The aim of this guide is to provide you with a clear understanding of the requirements of Unit 1 of the AS specification and to advise you on how best to meet these requirements.

This guide looks at:
- the psychology you need to know about
- what you need to be able to do and what skills you need
- how you could go about learning the necessary material
- what is being examined
- what you should expect in the examination
- how you could tackle the different styles of exam question
- the format of the exam, including what questions might look like
- how questions are marked, including examples of answers, with examiner's comments

### How to use this guide

A good way of using this guide is to read it through in the order in which it is presented. Alternatively, you can consider each topic in the Content Guidance section, and then turn to a relevant question in the Question and Answer section. Whichever way you use the guide, try some of the questions yourself to test your learning. Hopefully, you will know enough about the marking by this time to try to grade your own answers. If you are working with someone else, mark each other's answers. Working with someone else is more enjoyable and means you are actively learning. For example, try explaining the material to others, as this is an effective way of learning. The more you work on what is needed, the better. Have your textbooks available too — you will need access to all the relevant information.

Use a glossary of terms if you have one. Try testing yourself (or work with a friend) on main terms. If you know the terms you are at least halfway there, if not more.

# Study skills and revision strategies

If you have been studying the Unit 1 material, and have engaged in a reasonable amount of learning up to now, you can make good use of this guide.

This guide can also help if you know little of the material and have only a short time before the examination. If this describes you, you have a lot of work and long hours of study ahead — but you can do it.

*Before reading on, answer the following questions:*
- How long is left before the exam?
- Do you have a revision plan?
- Are you sure you want to pass and hopefully do well? Renewing your motivation can help.
- Are you stressed and in a panic?
- Can you stick to your plan and trust it?

If you need to, draw up a revision plan now, remind yourself that you want to succeed, and practise some relaxation techniques.

## How to learn the material
- Make notes, be concise and use your own notes for final revision.
- Have a separate sheet of paper for each approach.
- For each approach, note down the six headings (see the summary at the start of each approach) and use that as a guide. Leave room to fit your notes in under each heading.
- Read through each section, then make brief notes as needed.
- Be sure to make notes on evaluation points.
- Finally, note down briefly three things about a key issue that describe the issue, and six 'facts' linking concepts to the issue.

Another useful method is to use cards for each topic. Have the topic heading on one side of the card and brief notes on the other. Remember to note down equal amounts of knowledge and evaluation.

## Revision plan

- Start at least 4 weeks before the exam date (sooner if possible).
- Using times that suit you (6 a.m. might be a great time for you to study), draw up a blank timetable for each of the weeks.
- On the timetable, fill in all your urgent commitments (cancel as many plans as you can).
- Divide up what is left, allocating slots to all your subjects as appropriate. Don't forget to build in meal times, breaks and time for sleep.
- Stick to the plan if at all possible, but if you have to, amend it as you go.
- When studying, have frequent, short rests and no distractions.

## Time management

Answer the following questions to see how good you are at time management:

**(1)** Are you usually punctual?

yes      no

**(2)** Do you tend to work fast and then correct mistakes?

yes      no

**(3)** Do you often put things off?

yes      no

**(4)** Do you feel stressed because you never have enough time?

yes      no

**(5)** Do you work slowly and carefully, and try to get things right first time?

yes      no

**(6)** Do you daydream?

yes      no

**(7)** Are you forgetful?

yes      no

**(8)** Do you find it hard to get started?

yes      no

**(9)** Do you keep your desk tidy?

yes      no

Score 0 for 'yes' and 1 for 'no' to questions 1, 5 and 9. Score 1 for 'yes' and 0 for 'no' to questions 2, 3, 4, 6, 7 and 8. A score of 3 or below means quite good time management; a score of 4 and above means you need to work on it.

# Relaxation techniques

Boxes 1, 2 and 3 suggest ways to relax. Use these as appropriate.

---

**Box 1: Technique 1 — takes about 10 minutes**

This technique is useful at the start or at the end of a longish revision period.

- Sit or lie on the floor and make yourself comfortable.
- Working from toes to head, tense each of your muscles in turn and then relax.
- Having relaxed your body, now relax your thoughts.
- Take yourself in your mind to a place where you feel at peace — this could be a favourite holiday place or somewhere special on a walk. Closing your eyes will help.
- Have a good look around (mentally), sit down there and hear the sounds of the place.
- Stay there and try not to come back yet.
- When you are ready, come back. Slowly start to hear the sounds around you and sit or lie with your body relaxed for a little while longer.

---

**Box 2: Technique 2 — takes about 5 minutes**

This technique is useful as you revise. Work for between 30 minutes and an hour, and then stop to relax as follows:

- Sit comfortably and try to ignore anything going on around you.
- Imagine you are in a barn, high up on the rafters under the roof, swinging your legs and sitting comfortably. Closing your eyes will help.
- Now, imagine that the barn has open doors at both ends, and there is a river rushing through from one end to the other. You are sitting swinging your legs, watching the river rush through below you.
- Hear the water rushing through, sit comfortably and just watch.
- Think of the water as your thoughts rushing away.
- You are not involved, just watching.
- After about 3 minutes or when you are ready, slowly start to hear the sounds around you, and gradually bring your thoughts back into the real world.
- Look around you for a minute or two and check that you feel better, before getting back to work.

---

**Box 3: Technique 3 — takes about 1 minute**

This technique is useful when you are actually in the examination, and can be used if you are too anxious to continue.

- Imagine you are in an exam now.
- Imagine that you are getting anxious.
- Pick up a pen as if to write.
- Hold the pen up in front of you and stare at it.
- Let all your other thoughts go and think about the pen.
- Try to think of nothing else, even for a few seconds.
- Get back to work!

---

# Examination structure and skills

## Two approaches, six areas within each

Unit 1 consists of questions split into three different types ranging across the two approaches (Unit 2 consists of the same three different types of questions ranging across its three approaches).

The three different types of question are multiple-choice, short answer and extended answer questions. You will not know how many marks there are for each approach, but it is certain that both the Unit 1 approaches will be covered somewhere in the paper.

Within each approach there are six areas:
- key terms and the basics of the approach (definitions)
- methodology
- content
- two studies in detail
- a key issue
- a practical

The aim in the Unit 1 examination is to ask questions covering the six areas within the approaches, as well as the two approaches themselves.

For example, if you are asked a question about a key issue in the cognitive approach, you are unlikely to be asked a 'key issue' question for the social approach in the same examination.

Remember the six main areas: definitions, methodology, content, studies, key issue and practical. The two approaches for Unit 1 are the social approach and the cognitive approach. You need to be prepared to answer a question on any of the six main areas for each of the two approaches.

## Exam structure and assessment objectives (AOs)

Each of the two AS exam papers has multiple-choice questions at the start, followed by some short answer questions, some extended writing questions, and a 12-mark extended writing question (essay question) at the end.

The assessment objectives (AOs) of the AS exam papers are explained more fully below but can be briefly described as:
- **AO1** — testing knowledge with understanding and good communication skills
- **AO2** — testing evaluation, assessment and applications
- **AO3** — testing understanding and evaluation of methodology, including other people's studies

Don't think that someone sets each paper with past papers in front of them, avoiding what has been asked before. Imagine someone trying to set an interesting paper, covering the six areas, ranging across the approaches and balancing AO1, AO2 and AO3 marks according to the required percentages of each.

It is not possible to guess what will be on the paper — don't try. Prepare answers for all possible questions. The only guarantee is that there will be the three types of question (multiple choice, short answer and extended writing) and an essay question at the end of each paper; the mark allocation for that essay is 12 marks.

Different people set the papers, and there are not as many strict rules as you might think. Tips in this guide include words such as 'usually'. Each paper will be different, and you have to be prepared to answer whatever questions appear. For example, there are many ways that short answer questions can be written, such as:

- 'Explain what is meant by...'
- 'Describe the procedure of...'
- 'Outline the theory...'
- 'Outline two weaknesses of...'
- 'What is the hypothesis in this study...?'

Read the question carefully and do what is asked, and you will do well.

## Assessment objectives

The assessment objectives are listed in the specification. A brief explanation is given below, but check the full list of what you will be assessed on.

### Assessment objective 1: knowledge and understanding (AO1)

- You need to recognise, recall and show understanding of psychological knowledge, including theories, studies, methods and concepts, as well as psychological principles, perspectives and applications.
- You must communicate clearly and effectively, presenting and selecting material well. For example, if you are asked to explain what is meant by obedience for 3 marks, and you just say that it is about obeying, you have not explained anything. You need to make your points clearly — for example:

'Obedience is about following the orders of someone in authority and can be explained by saying that someone is in an agentic state when they follow such orders. An example might be the obedience shown in Milgram's main study, when participants thought they were giving someone electric shocks and they continued, even though it clearly distressed them.'

- You may lose marks by using bullet points, so avoid them. The problem with bullet points is that they encourage shorthand, meaning that your answer will not be clearly and effectively communicated.

### Assessment objective 2: evaluation and comment (AO2)

You must be able to:

- analyse and evaluate psychological theories and concepts, referring to relevant evidence
- apply psychological knowledge and understanding to unfamiliar situations
- assess the validity, reliability and credibility of psychological knowledge

*Assessment objective 3 (AO3)*

You must be able to:

- describe ethical, safe and skilful practical techniques and processes, including selecting appropriate qualitative and quantitative methods
- know how to make, record and communicate reliable and valid measurement, using primary and secondary sources
- analyse, explain, interpret and evaluate the methodology, results and impact of both your own practicals and the studies of others

# The Unit 1 exam

Unit 1 is assessed in an 80-minute exam. Answers are written in a booklet similar to those used at GCSE. 60 marks are available. This means you need to score around 1 mark per minute, with 20 minutes to spare for reading and thinking. In general, you can expect to gain 1 mark for each point that answers the question, or for elaboration of a point.

Answers must be communicated 'clearly and effectively' (see AO1 above). Avoid one-word answers unless they are asked for.

The final essay question is worth 12 marks.

Overall:

- One-third of the marks (around 20 marks) are awarded for knowledge and under-standing (AO1).
- One-third (around 20 marks) are for evaluation and comment and application to unfamiliar situations (AO2).
- One-third (around 20 marks) are for knowing about and assessing practical work, both your own and other people's.

With regard to the split over the type of questions, about 18% (around 11 marks) are involved in multiple-choice questions, about 50% (around 30 marks) involve short answer questions and the remaining 32% (around 19 marks) involve extended writing, including the 12-mark essay question at the end.

In practice you can just focus on revising equal amounts of AO1, AO2 and AO3 (know-ledge, evaluation and practical work) and just answer each question as it arises.

## Two types of marking

There are two types of marking. One type is point-based marking, where 1 mark per point made is awarded, and also there are marks for elaboration and saying more about a point. The other type of marking is called 'levels'. In this type, bands of marks are awarded according to the quality of the answer.

For example, the mark scheme for a question asking for the independent variable (IV) for one of your studies for 2 marks:

- 0 marks — no appropriate material, e.g. giving the dependent variable (DV).
- 1 mark — not fully operationalised, such as giving one side of the IV.

- 2 marks — fully operationalised, giving both or all sides of the IV. Possibly an example is given.

Questions about your own practicals are marked according to levels and the quality — for example, if you are asked about planning your questionnaire, a thorough answer will get full marks and a weak answer will get few marks.

The essays are also marked using levels and according to quality. For example, if you are asked about two explanations for gender development and you only discuss one explanation, you will be somewhere in the middle band.

It is in the levels marking that your written skills are assessed, including how well you select material for your answer and what your spelling, grammar and use of terminology are like.

## AO1, AO2 and AO3: getting it right

You must be sure to answer the question that is set — you should then cover the AO1, AO2 and/or AO3 skills.

The key words in the question (called **injunctions**, e.g. 'outline') guide what you need to write. If you answer the question, you will do what is required without worrying about the various assessment objectives.

Table 1 shows some examples of how AO1 injunctions are used and Table 2 shows examples of AO2 injunctions. Table 3 shows some examples of AO3 questions, which can include all sorts of injunctions but must be about practicals and methodology in some way.

Note that it is not so much the word itself (e.g. 'describe') that makes it AO1, AO2, or AO3, as the whole question.

The figures in brackets suggest the mark allocation you might expect for such a question.

### Table 1 Examples of AO1 questions/injunctions

| Type of question | What is being asked for |
|---|---|
| Describe a theory… (4) | Say what something is (a theory in this case). Imagine describing the theory to someone who knows little about the subject. |
| Identify a theory… (1) | Give enough information to enable the examiner to understand what is being referred to. For example, if you are asked to identify a memory theory, the answer might be 'working memory model'. |
| Name a theory… (1) | Name either the theory or the psychologist(s). For example, if the question asks for a memory theory, the answer might be Atkinson and Shiffrin's or the two-stage model. |
| Outline a definition of the…approach (2) | Follow the instructions for 'describe', but remember that this injunction requires less detail, and hence carries fewer marks. |
| Describe Hofling et al.'s (1966) study… (5) | Try to give the aim of the study, the method, the procedure, the results and the conclusion(s). |

*Table 2 Examples of AO2 questions/injunctions*

| Type of question | What is being asked for |
|---|---|
| Outline a strength of... (2) | You are asked to outline something, so the injunction seems to be AO1 (knowledge and understanding). However, as what is outlined is a strength (in this case), and thus you are being asked to evaluate something, this question would carry AO2 marks. |
| With regard to the stimulus material above, explain... (6) | You are asked to refer to some stimulus material and apply your knowledge of psychology to explain the material in some way. Refer to the material at least once in your answer. |
| Compare two theories of memory... (6) | You are asked to choose two theories of memory and then write about how they are similar and/or how they are different. And/or means you can do both or one or the other. |
| Assess how far cue-dependent forgetting is a useful theory... (4) | You are asked to consider practical uses of the theory of forgetting or you can evaluate the theory itself, because that would shed light on how useful it might be — but focus on its usefulness. |

*Table 3 Examples of AO3 questions/injunctions*

| Type of question | What is being asked for |
|---|---|
| Outline the aim(s) of your experiment... (2) | You are asked to say what the purpose of your study was, which is to say briefly what you were trying to find out. 'Outline' sounds like an AO1 injunction, but as this is about your practical, it is an AO3 question. |
| Evaluate one of these studies — either Reicher and Haslam (2006), Tafjel et al. (1970) or Sherif et al. (1954) the Robber's Cave study... (5) | You will have covered one of these studies but not all of them. Choose the one you know and give comments, criticisms, good points and so on about it. Consider the strengths and weaknesses of the research method, perhaps, or criticisms of the ethics involved. Look at alternative findings or consider whether justified conclusions are drawn. This is an AO3 question, even though 'evaluate' sounds like an AO2 injunction. It is about someone else's study, which is psychology in practice, so it is an AO3 question. Reicher and Haslam is explained in this guide. |

## Conclusions: use of injunctions and the AO1/AO2/AO3 split

Don't just think of a word in the question as being the whole question. For example, you would think 'describe' is an AO1 command because it seems to ask for knowledge, but 'describe a strength' is an AO2 injunction because it asks for evaluation. And 'describe the procedure of your practical' is an AO3 question because it asks about psychology in practice.

'Discuss' could signal AO2 marks if you are asked to 'discuss the usefulness of...'. Because you are considering how useful something is, you are doing more than showing knowledge about it. The best approach is to *answer the question*. If you study the question and understand the question, all should be well.

# Content
# Guidance

This section provides an overview of what you need to learn for Unit 1. Remember, you need access to more material than is given here.

An attempt is made here to balance presenting knowledge with giving suggestions for evaluation, whether about psychology itself (AO1 and AO2) or about psychology in practice (AO3). Remember to prepare for AO1, AO2 and AO3 questions.

## Structure of the AS units

Unit 1 comprises the social and cognitive approaches to psychology. Unit 2 is about three more approaches — the psychodynamic approach, the biological approach and the learning approach.

Each approach follows the same format:
- definition and some specified key terms
- methodology (specified)
- content (some specified, some choice)
- two studies in detail (one specified and one other from a particular choice)
- one key issue (your choice)
- one practical (your choice — research method and some issues specified)

# The social approach

Unit 1 covers the social and the cognitive approaches. This section looks at the social approach. For some areas of Unit 1 you can choose what you study. In this section suitable material is presented, but you may have studied different examples. *You might be better advised to revise the material you chose for your course.* However, you can choose what is summarised in the box below.

### *Summary of the social approach*

**Definition and key terms**

The approach is defined in this section, and key terms are listed and briefly explained. The key terms are defined where they appear in the Content Guidance section.

**Methodology**

The survey method, including questionnaires and interviews, is outlined, together with an evaluation. Qualitative and quantitative data, both used in surveys, are outlined as well, again with evaluation. Four sampling techniques are covered, as are five ethical issues in 'doing' psychology.

**Content**

Obedience is defined and agency theory — which is a way of understanding obedience — is explained. Milgram's (a main figure in the field of obedience) main study and variations are outlined (you need to know one), with evaluation and consideration of ethics. Meeus and Raijmakers's study (a study of obedience in another country) is outlined and evaluated too and comparisons are made to consider cultural differences. The social identity theory of prejudice is explained, with definitions of prejudice and discrimination.

**Two studies in detail**

Hofling et al. (1966) and Reicher and Haslam (2003/6) are described and evaluated. You may have studied Tajfel's work or Sherif's study instead.

**Key issue**

The issue of blind obedience in a prison setting (Abu Ghraib) is covered, but you may have looked at one or more different key issues.

**Practical**

You will have carried out at least one practical within social psychology and you should use your own practical, because you will have 'learned by doing'. Some ideas about the practical are suggested in this book.

# Definition and key terms

The social approach is about people both as individuals and as part of a group or groups. It is about how people live together comfortably, and when they do not, as well as about social structures — who obeys, who gives orders. Questions considered in social psychology include why people obey, why people help or do not help others, why people are attracted to certain people, and why some people are aggressive, for example in crowds.

**Exam preparation**  Prepare an answer for 6 marks defining social psychology, including two examples.

Key terms you need to know: agentic state, autonomous state, moral strain, in-group, out-group, social categorisation, social identification, social comparison. These are dealt with in the content section below.

**Exam preparation**  Prepare an answer for 3 marks defining each key term and including one example each time.

# Methodology

## Why methodology is important

Methodology concerns how psychology is carried out — the main point being to ensure that findings (results and conclusions) are secure. 'Secure' involves various issues that are evaluation points, such as **validity**, **reliability**, **generalisability**, **objectivity**, **credibility** — and there are other important evaluation issues, such as ethical issues. To get 'secure' data, the methodology of a study is carefully planned. This is what the methodology sections in your course are about. Methodology is the study of the way a study is carried out.

*Key methodology evaluation terms*

| Methodology evaluation term | Explanation |
|---|---|
| Validity | Measuring what you claim to measure, meaning that what you measure is 'real life' and not something forced because of the study's methodology. |
| Reliability | Getting the same results if you do a study again, because if you do not get the same results, the data are not worth much. To test for reliability there needs to be **replicability** (the study has to be capable of being repeated). |
| Generalisability | The sampling is such that results can be said to be true of other people that the study is meant to represent. |
| Objectivity/subjectivity | The study is not biased because of the researcher giving their own opinions or influencing the results. Controls, for example, help to keep a study objective. Subjectivity is what occurs when the researcher affects the results with their own views. |
| Credibility | When the findings (results and conclusions) of a study are explained, people accept them. The data seem believable (credible). The methodology is also sound. |

**Exam preparation**  List the above key methodology evaluation terms and define each for 2 marks.

# Basic methodological features of a study

A study will have an **aim** and most studies will have a **hypothesis**. There are **variables**, and for most studies there will be an **independent variable (IV)** and a **dependent variable (DV)**, both of which have to be carefully **operationalised**. Generally, there are **controls** over other variables, such as **situational variables** and **participant variables**. These are key methodology description terms.

*Key methodology description terms*

| Methodology description term | Explanation |
|---|---|
| Aim | A brief statement of what the study is intending to find, such as 'to see if people are more hostile to someone who is not a member of their own group'. |
| Hypothesis (alternative) | A carefully defined statement of what the study is aiming to find. The IV and the DV are both clearly stated, saying exactly what is being done and what is being measured. The social approach talks about the alternative hypothesis, which is the overall term for the statement. (Then there is an experimental hypothesis — for experiments — and a null hypothesis, explained later.) |
| Operationalising | Making something measurable and clear. For example, to study the aim given here, hostility has to be measured somehow, as does what the in-group and the out-group are. This is done by operationalising the variables — making them measurable. |
| Independent variable (IV) | The variable that the researcher manipulates (changes) to see the effect on the dependent variable. For example, a study could look at whether two people act differently depending on whether they belong to the same group or to two different groups. The IV is whether they belong to the same group (in-group) or to two different groups (out-group). |
| Conditions | An IV has more than one condition, as it is about the different way that X or Y would affect the DV. There are often two conditions, such as in the example used here, where one condition is the in-group (people in your group) and the other is the out-group (people not in your group). |
| Dependent variable (DV) | The variable that is measured to see the effect of the IV. In the example about in-group/out-group behaviour the DV was 'act differently', and that would have to be operationalised. For example, saying nice things about the in-group members and unpleasant things about the out-group members, as measured by questionnaire. |
| Control | The IV is changed and the DV measured, but everything else is controlled to make sure nothing else affects the results. For example, making sure that not all the in-group are female and the out-group male, otherwise you might find hostility to the out-group because of gender differences, not because they are 'out-group'. Controls are put in place to keep everything the same except for the IV/DV. |
| Situational variables | Variables in the situation such as noise, temperature and light might affect the results if they are different in the different conditions. |
| Participant variables | Variables in the participants such as mood, hunger, age or gender might affect the results if they are different in the different conditions. |

17

List the above key terms and define each for 2 marks. Be able to give an example of each, as is done in the table. You could use your own practical to give the examples, as that would help your revision of your practical as well.

# Research methods

Methodology is all about the methods used in psychology to gather data. A number of main research methods are used, within which different methodological issues arise. Research methods you will cover include surveys, which comprise questionnaires and interviews; experiments, which include field, laboratory and natural experiments; case studies and observations. Each approach focuses on different research methods (as well as different aspects of methodology).

*Approaches (Unit 1 and Unit 2) and related research method*

| Approach | Main research method focused on |
|---|---|
| Social | Survey (questionnaires and interviews) |
| Cognitive | Experiments (laboratory, field and natural) |
| Psychodynamic | Case studies (including Freud's style of case study) |
| Biological | General testing |
| Learning | Observations |

## Questionnaires

Questionnaires gather **personal data** because the researcher needs to know something about the **respondent** (the person answering). But only necessary data should be gathered. For example, if you do not need to know someone's job, do not ask.

Then there are questions that extract the other data required. For example, if the aim is to see if people are more hostile to someone who is not a member of their own group, the questionnaire needs to find out about people's attitudes to people in groups to which they belong and people in other groups.

There are many different ways of asking such questions, such as using a **Likert-type scale** (strongly agree, agree, don't know, disagree, strongly disagree), or any other rating scale. Questions can simply ask for 'yes' or 'no' answers. Other questions can ask directly for someone's opinion, such as 'What do you think about...?'

### Closed questions

Closed questions are those where the answer is a forced choice — the respondent has no chance of giving any answer other than the choice given. An example of a closed question (sometimes called a closed-ended question) is a question asking for the answer 'yes' or 'no'.

### Strengths and weaknesses of closed-ended questions

| Strengths | Weaknesses |
|---|---|
| ● Generate standard replies that can be counted for ease of comparability and analysis | ● Force a choice of answer (even 'unsure') so may not give the answer respondents would prefer, so they are not valid |
| ● Same clearly expressed, detailed questions, so if repeated tend to get the same responses; reliable | ● 'Unsure' can mean 'don't know' or 'sometimes yes and sometimes no'; answers may mean different things to different respondents, so they are not comparable |

*Open questions*

Open questions leave the answer open for the respondent to give their views. An example of an open question (sometimes called an open-ended question) is a question asking 'What do you think about...?'

### Strengths and weaknesses of open-ended questions

| Strengths | Weaknesses |
|---|---|
| ● Respondent is not constrained but free to answer as they wish, so will give more detailed, in-depth and rich data | ● Difficult to analyse because tend to be interpreted by the respondent; too difficult to compare data with those of other respondents |
| ● Allows respondent to interpret the questions as they wish, so produces more valid 'real' data than when constrained by the questions | ● Often are not answered in full as they take longer and it is more difficult to think of the answer than when ticking a forced-choice box |

*Quantitative data*

Quantitative data are data where numbers are collected and given scores. For example, if time is measured, that is quantitative, or if the number of 'yes' answers and the number of 'no' answers are counted, that is quantitative. Closed questions gather quantitative data. Even categories like 'strongly agree' involve scoring.

### Likert-type scale and scoring

**SA: strongly agree; A: agree; DK: unsure; D: disagree; SD: strongly disagree**

| Statement | SA | A | DK | D | SD |
|---|---|---|---|---|---|
| I don't talk much with people outside my own group | 5 | 4 | 3 | 2 | 1 |
| I have lots of friends with the same interests | 5 | 4 | 3 | 2 | 1 |
| I like meeting people even if they are different from me | 1 | 2 | 3 | 4 | 5 |

The table is scored 'high' for 'prefers own in-group'.

*Qualitative data*

Qualitative data are data about opinions and attitudes rather than numbers. They are data that tell a story in some way. Open questions gather qualitative data when they ask questions such as 'What do you think of people who do not have the same ideas as you?'

### Strengths and weaknesses of qualitative data

| Strengths | Weaknesses |
|---|---|
| • Allow more in-depth analysis because of greater detail | • Difficult to analyse because the data can be so different that they are hard to summarise |
| • More valid because respondents can say what they really think | • There is more detail and depth and it can take longer both for the researcher and the participant |

A questionnaire usually includes both open and closed questions and so gathers both quantitative (giving quantity) and qualitative (giving quality) data. A **pilot survey** is useful. This is a survey run with a few participants to test the questions and check their clarity and suitability. In the light of the pilot, changes can be made.

**Exam preparation**  Define the terms — open question, closed question, quantitative data and qualitative data. Then write a paragraph linking the four terms. Finally, note one strength and one weakness of each.

*Collecting data using questionnaires*

Questionnaires can be posted out to people, which can be quite costly and also risks producing a low response rate. However, a lot of people can be reached that way and more have the opportunity to take part. The sample would be a volunteer sample — of those who were sent the questionnaire in the first place. The questionnaires can be handed out by the researcher and completed there and then, which should improve the response rate but would limit the coverage. They can be handed out by someone else or left somewhere for completion. All these different ways of getting data mean that this is a flexible research method.

*Analysis of quantitative data/closed questions*

Quantitative data provide numbers, so initial analysis is by means of percentages and descriptive statistics. **Descriptive statistics** include **measures of central tendency**, which are the mode, median and mean averages. Graphs are also used, such as bar charts, line graphs and pie charts. The data are analysed in such a way that they can be clearly displayed and understood. Sometimes just totals are used.

**Mode** — the most common score in the set of scores:

1  5  7  8  8  12  12  12  15 — the mode is 12

**Median** — the middle score in the set of scores:

1  5  7  8  8  12  12  12  15 — the median is 8

1   5   7   8   8   11   13   14   15   20 — the median is 9.5 (between 8 and 11)

**Mean** — the arithmetical average found by totalling all the scores in the set and dividing by the number of scores in the set:

1   5   7   8   8   11   13   14   15   20 — the mean is 10.2 (102 divided by 10)

### Analysis of qualitative data/open questions

Qualitative data are in the form of a story or comments from the respondent, so need to be summarised in some way to make them manageable and clear. This is done by generating themes from the data, such as finding that most respondents comment on liking people of the same age or on not liking people from a different social class. Themes would focus on age and class.

### Analysis of questionnaires

Using the quantitative data, scores are assigned to groups obtained from the personal data. For example, scores of males and females can be separated and compared. Scores of younger and older respondents can be compared, or scores of those employed compared to those of students. This rather depends on the hypothesis/aim of the questionnaire.

The themes from the qualitative data can also be sorted into groups such as gender, age and class, depending on what the researcher wants to find out. Perhaps, for example, males talk more about class and females talk more about age.

> **Exam preparation**   In one paragraph each, summarise how you would analyse quantitative data, qualitative data and questionnaires so that you can answer a question in each case about how to analyse them.

### Evaluation of questionnaires as a research method

*Evaluate using the type of question and type of data*

When evaluating questionnaires, you can use evaluation of the types of question (open and closed) and the types of data (qualitative and quantitative).

Open questions gather qualitative data, which are useful because they provide rich detail that can generate themes and give more in-depth analysis. Closed questions gather quantitative data, which are useful because analysis can be in the form of percentages and averages, numbers that can be compared more easily than themes.

*Evaluate by looking at validity*

Questionnaires can be evaluated according to their validity, which means how far what they gather is 'real-life' information.

When someone has to answer a question that has a forced choice of response (such as yes/no questions) they are restricted in their answer, so their responses are not likely to be valid. They might want to say something else entirely. This is a lack of **construct validity** (the questions don't do a good job of measuring what they are supposed to measure).

When someone is answering a questionnaire, they are doing an artificial task and so are in an artificial situation. This means the responses lack **ecological validity** (the answers are not given in a setting or situation that is natural to the respondent, so they may not be valid because of that).

Questionnaires can only find out what the respondents think is true of themselves or how they would behave. They do not measure actual behaviour. So there is a lack of validity in this sense as well.

To an extent questionnaires are valid when they use open questions because then the respondent has some chance of saying what they 'really' think — though you could argue that given lack of space and the demands of the question, this validity is limited.

Issues affecting validity include how truthful the answers are. It is hard to know this, but some issues affect truthfulness more than others, so an attempt is made at trying to avoid these issues. **Demand characteristics** are when characteristics of a question or features of any study (demand characteristics are found in other research methods too) give clues to the respondent or participant about the answer(s) expected. Questions need to be subtle and to hide their true intention (while remembering ethical issues, which are discussed below). **Social desirability** can also affect answers, as people tend to reply as they think they should reply. For example, if asked if you are a racist, you are unlikely to say yes.

*Evaluate by looking at reliability*
Questionnaires can be evaluated by considering how reliable they are. This means considering whether, if the questionnaire were carried out again, the same results would be found.

A pilot study would test questions for ease of understanding and usefulness with regard to achieving the questionnaire's aims, so that would help reliability. If the questions are clear, the same findings are likely to be produced if they are administered again.

Closed questions have forced-choice answers, so respondents are likely to fit themselves into the same category if asked again. This means questionnaires are a reasonably reliable method.

Questionnaires are set out and repeated exactly — they are replicable, which is a condition for reliability.

Open questions might be less reliable, as they allow for opinions to be given and opinions may differ over time and place. In one mood a respondent might answer one way, whereas in another state they might answer differently.

*Evaluate by looking at generalisability*
Generalisability depends on how well the sampling ensures that the people asked represent the population that is being looked at (the target population). In your course

you look at random sampling, stratified sampling, volunteer/self-selected sampling and opportunity sampling. To help you to understand these four types of sampling, as well as to understand issues of generalisability, those four are considered here with regard to questionnaires. Results are **generalisable** when they come from good sampling that represents the target population, so it can be said that what was found is 'true' of all the others who were not in the sample.

(1) **Random sampling** means that everyone in the target population or sampling frame has an equal chance of being picked to be in the sample. The target population is likely to be very large (such as everyone if you are looking at memory, perhaps), but random sampling of everyone is not possible, as not all of them would be available to be picked. The sampling frame is those who can be picked, such as all students in one sixth form, and all of those would need to be available to be chosen if the sample is random. (Two ways of doing this are names in a hat, or using random number tables and a list of all the names.) A random sample gives good generalisability because you would expect the sample to be representative of the target population and not to have bias.

(2) **Stratified sampling** means generating categories that fit the aim(s) of the study, such as age, gender, occupation, or whether someone drives or not. From these categories people are chosen, so that the sample is bound to include people from these categories. This can be generalisable because all the necessary characteristics will be in the sample, though the numbers in each category should reflect the numbers in the target population, which is not easy to do.

(3) **Volunteer/self-selected sampling** means asking people to volunteer. If a questionnaire is sent out by post, those returning it will by definition have volunteered. It is not easy to generalise from this, because there is something different about people who volunteer and select themselves for the sample. They might have strong views about the topic, for example, or have more time than other people.

(4) **Opportunity sampling** means the researcher takes whoever they can find. This can be biased because it would be anyone around at that time, which might exclude those working or those at school if the study was done on a weekday in the daytime. It is not easy to generalise from such sampling, because there is no science in how people are obtained and there is a strong element of chance and bias.

*Strengths and weaknesses of simple random sampling*

| Strengths | Weaknesses |
|---|---|
| • Low bias because everyone has an equal chance of being chosen | • Cannot be certain that the sample is representative of all groups/types etc. |
| • Sample can be checked mathematically for bias | • Difficult to access all the population so that random sampling can take place |

### Strengths and weaknesses of stratified sampling

| Strengths | Weaknesses |
| --- | --- |
| • All relevant groups/strata will have at least some representation | • It is difficult to know how many of each group is needed in order to represent the target population accurately |
| • Limits the numbers of participants needed | • Relies on researchers knowing all the required groups/strata; forces choice of participants and proportions of all groups so can give bias by excluding people |

### Strengths and weaknesses of volunteer/self-selected sampling

| Strengths | Weaknesses |
| --- | --- |
| • Ethically good because people volunteer, so are willing to be involved | • Only certain types of people may volunteer, so there is bias |
| • More likely to cooperate, which means there may be less social desirability and such biases | • May take a long time to get enough volunteers |

### Strengths and weaknesses of opportunity sampling

| Strengths | Weaknesses |
| --- | --- |
| • More ethical because the researcher can judge if the participant is likely to be upset by the study or is too busy to take part | • Only people available are used and they may be a self-selected group (e.g. not working, so available during the day) |
| • The researcher has more control over who is chosen and should, therefore, be able to get the sample quickly and efficiently | • May not get representatives from all groups so there may be bias |

*Evaluate by looking at objectivity*

Psychology is a science and as such needs to present data that are reliable and objective. Objectivity refers to avoiding bias when gathering data, particularly bias from the researcher's own opinions and understanding. Controls are used to make sure data are objectively gathered. Controls have to cover situational and participant variables. **Experimenter/researcher effects** must also be controlled for, such as the effects of tone of voice, clothes worn or the gender or age of the researcher. This is important in a questionnaire. Subjectivity is to be avoided (there must be objectivity for research to be scientific, which is an aim of psychology) when data are analysed as well as when data are gathered. For example, when themes are being generated these must come from the data, not from preconceptions of the researcher.

*Evaluate by looking at credibility*

Science must generate credible data. If psychology maintains that something is true which people do not believe, this is not useful. Data are credible if they are valid (true to life) and reliable (found more than once). They are credible if they can be generalised (said to be true of others, not just the sample used) and if they agree with common sense. If the evidence is carefully presented and strong, the results will be believed (they will be credible) — usually. There are occasions when psychology puts forward a finding that is 'incredible' — such as Milgram's finding that 'ordinary' people were capable of doing 'extraordinary' things (giving what they thought were lethal electric shocks to others). If the evidence is strong enough (which Milgram's was) and relates to real life (which it did, because in the Holocaust 'ordinary' people did 'extraordinary' things), the findings are accepted in spite of their apparent lack of credibility.

#### Strengths and weaknesses of questionnaires

| Strengths | Weaknesses |
|---|---|
| • They are often reliable because bias from the researcher can be avoided by having set questions and a set procedure | • They could be administered differently by different people, so data may be biased by the situation, which would make them unreliable |
| • If questions and procedure are set so that bias is avoided, data should be valid | • If fixed questions are mainly asked then useful relevant data can be missed, making data invalid. Respondents are not free to say what they want to say, even if open questions are chosen |

*Evaluation using ethical considerations*

In your course you have studied five main ethical guidelines — informed consent, lack of deceit, right to withdraw, debriefing and competence.

#### Five main ethical guidelines for your course

| Guideline | Explanation |
|---|---|
| Informed consent | Participants must agree to taking part and having their data used, knowing as much as possible about the study (they consent, and it is informed consent). |
| Deceit | There must be no deceit — participants must be fully informed. Where deceit is necessary because otherwise the study would not work, there must be a full debrief. |
| Right to withdraw | Participants must be given the right to withdraw at any time, both during the study and afterwards, when they can withdraw their data. |
| Debrief | Participants must be fully informed after the study — of what it was about and where their findings fit. This is particularly important if there is deceit and, therefore, lack of informed consent. |
| Competence | The researcher must be competent to carry out the study. They must be sufficiently qualified and/or overseen by someone else. They must adhere to ethical guidelines and understand not only what they are doing, but also the consequences, which they must be equipped to deal with. |

Questionnaires can have good ethics, because ethical considerations can be addressed on the questionnaire itself. The right to withdraw can be clearly stated, for example, as can the purpose of the study. Participants can usually be fully informed and not deceived. A debrief can also be included at the end in written form, or the researcher can explain after collecting the data. The questionnaire can be checked to make sure it is suitable and ethical, which ensures competence, although the consequences of completing the questionnaire must be considered (for example, if the topic is potentially distressing).

Later in this section, when Milgram's work is considered, you can practise using the five ethical issues in preparation for the examination.

## Interviews

Surveys can be carried out using interviews as well as questionnaires. You will have looked at three types of interviews — structured, semi-structured and unstructured interviews.

*Table to show three types of interview and brief evaluation*

| Type of interview | Explanation | Brief evaluation |
|---|---|---|
| Structured | Planned questions throughout | + Can be repeated and data can be compared<br>– Forced choice, so tends to lack validity |
| Semi-structured | Half planned, half able to explore issues | + More valid, as can explore to get real-life answers<br>– Can be hard to compare data if issues different |
| Unstructured | Areas planned but questions can follow lead of respondent — looser structure | + More valid, as respondent leads<br>– Less comparable and less replicable — harder to test for reliability |

A structured interview is essentially a questionnaire administered individually. An unstructured interview is much looser in format and the interviewer can explore issues. A semi-structured interview draws on both these ideas. In general, data from interviews are qualitative data, although the structured part of the interview is likely to gather quantitative data, and personal data (age, gender etc.) tend to generate quantitative data.

Interviews need a **schedule**, which is the set of questions/areas that need to be covered, whether in a fully structured or unstructured way. There also needs to be a **transcript,** which means writing out all the replies so that data can be thoroughly (and objectively) analysed.

When answering questions about interviews, with regard to open and closed questions, qualitative and quantitative data, and analysis of data, use what you have learned about these issues when looking at questionnaires, as the same issues arise. There might, however, be more bias in an interview because the interviewer can feature more, so there might be researcher effects.

*Strengths and weaknesses of interviews*

| Strengths | Weaknesses |
|---|---|
| • Questions can be explained and enlarged upon, so this is a good method when in-depth and detailed data are required | • The interviewer may influence the data (e.g. by tone, dress, gender), which would result in researcher bias |
| • Data tend to be valid because interviewees use their own words and are not as constrained by the questions as they are in a questionnaire | • Analysis may be subjective (e.g. generating themes) and the researcher's views may influence the analysis |

*Comparing questionnaires and interviews in terms of reliability, validity and subjectivity*

| Questionnaires | Interviews |
|---|---|
| **Reliability** Structured questions; the same for all respondents; so replicable and likely to be reliable | Each person interviewed separately in different settings and on different occasions and perhaps by a different person; difficult to replicate and test for reliability |
| **Validity** Set questions with forced-choice answers are likely to be less valid as may not yield 'true' data | Questions can be explained and explored, so likely to be valid and give 'real-life' and 'true' data |
| **Subjectivity** Structured format; less open to researcher bias in the analysis; closed questions do not require interpretation; open questions are likely to give short answers, so themes are clearer | Open to bias in analysis as generating themes requires interpretation; open to subjectivity, but analysis can be objective if the steps are made clear |

**Exam preparation** Compare questionnaires and interviews as research methods, in terms of descriptions of each. Then compare them in terms of evaluation of each, considering the issues of validity, reliability and subjectivity. Prepare enough to answer a question worth 8 marks in each case.

# Content

Within the social approach your course covers obedience and prejudice. Here these issues are dealt with in that order.

## Obedience

Obedience means to obey a direct order from an authority figure: an example is a soldier obeying orders. Conformity is different — it means you *agree* with carrying out out the action. Obedience and compliance both mean following orders when you do not necessarily agree.

A main name in the study of obedience is Milgram. He carried out a number of studies, the main one of which was in 1963, where he ordered participants to 'shock' someone. You need to know his basic study and at least one of the variations of that study.

## Milgram's 1963 basic study

### Aim

Milgram aimed to test the idea that 'Germans were different' when they carried out orders to persecute Jews and others during the Second World War. How far would 'ordinary people' go if ordered to administer what they thought were electric shocks to someone else? (He found that Germans are not different — others obeyed 'shocking' orders too.)

### Procedure

Through an advertisement 40 men were obtained who were willing to take part. The laboratory experiment took place at Yale, a well-regarded university. There was a room with a generator and levers. The levers had labels showing a range of voltages from 15 volts upwards and indicating from mild to severe shock and 'danger'. In another room was a chair that appeared to be wired up. The implication was clear — the generator delivered shocks and the person in the chair received the voltage on the label. There was an accomplice, whom the participants thought was another volunteer. The accomplice was placed in the chair and 'wired up'. He was primed to shout out at certain points, and then to go (ominously) quiet. In the meantime, the participant, who thought that he had been chosen as a 'teacher' and that the accomplice was just the 'learner' by chance (although in fact the draw was rigged), was seated at the generator and told what to do. The participant had to read out word pairs, which the accomplice had to 'learn' and be tested on. The accomplice, of course, was told to answer incorrectly sometimes, so that the teacher had to give 'shocks'. The teacher was told to increase the 'shock' by 15 volts at each wrong answer. The accomplice could be heard and not seen. The participant started the experiment and duly administered the shocks. Each participant was tested separately. If the participant protested and stopped, the experimenter said things like 'You must go on.' These instructions were called 'verbal prods'. After the fourth prod, if the participant still refused to go on, the experiment was stopped. After a time the accomplice was silent — he could have been injured or even be dead.

*Some main issues in the procedure*

| Issue | Comment |
|---|---|
| The participants were volunteers | This made the sample biased — look at strengths and weaknesses of volunteer samples as outlined earlier. |
| The participants were deceived | They were told it was a study of memory but it was about obedience. They were told that the accomplice was another participant, but he was not. They were told that the 'shocks' were real and they were not. |

| Issue | Comment |
|---|---|
| The participants were not given the right to withdraw fully | They could stop but there were four prods first, which is not in accordance with current guidelines. |
| The experimenter was in the room | They may have felt obliged to continue just because the experimenter was present — and supposedly making sure no harm was done to the 'accomplice'. |
| The study was at Yale University | This is a well-known university with a lot of prestige. The participants would expect things to be under control. |

## Results

Participants protested — but there was a script, and each time they protested the experimenter followed this script. All of them (100%) went up to 300 volts. Then some stopped and would not go on. However, 26 of the 40 men (65%) carried on to the end, which was 450 volts. During the study many participants were very distressed and one even had what was called a full-blown seizure.

## Conclusions

Milgram concluded that an ordinary person would obey orders from an authority to an extreme extent even when they were very uncomfortable about doing so.

> **Exam preparation**   Prepare enough for 2 marks for the aim, 6 marks for the procedure, 4 marks for the results and 4 marks for conclusions for each study you are covering, including Milgram's 1963 study. Then prepare enough for 4 marks on strengths and 4 marks on weaknesses so that you can evaluate a study when asked. Do that for Milgram's 1963 study now.

### *Strengths and weaknesses of the basic study by Milgram (1963)*

| Strengths | Weaknesses |
|---|---|
| • Good controls avoid bias and mean that the situation was the same for all, so cause-and-effect conclusions could be drawn | • The study is unethical because the participants were deceived, did not give informed consent, were distressed and did not have the full right to withdraw |
| • The well-controlled procedures mean that the study is replicable and can be tested for reliability | • The study lacks validity because of the artificial procedures |

# Variations of Milgram's 1963 study

You need to know one of the variations of the main study, which had the highest level of obedience (65%).

## Aims of variations

Milgram wanted to investigate reasons for the high level of obedience in a systematic way, so he changed one variable at a time to see what the effect was. Each variation had a separate aim which was to see:

- the effect of the study being at Yale, a prestigious university
- the effect of the victim being remote from the participant
- the effect of the experimenter being in the room
- what would happen if others were there, and they refused at some stage
- what would happen if there were two experimenters, one of whom told the participant to stop

**Procedures and results of variations**
- Moving the study to a run-down office block gave 47.5% obedience to 450 volts.
- Having the participant hold down the victim's hand to receive the shock gave 30% obedience to 450 volts.
- Not having the experimenter in the room and orders given over the phone, gave 22.5% obedience to 450 volts.
- Having two colleagues who both refused before 300 volts meant only 10% obedience to 450 volts.
- When one experimenter told the participant to stop and the other said continue, none of the participants continued to 450 volts.

**Exam preparation**   Make sure you can describe one of Milgram's variations as well as evaluate it.

# Agency theory

Milgram suggested that participants in his studies were in an agentic state, which means they acted as agents of the experimenter even though they were under moral strain. Moral strain refers to the pressure of doing something against one's feelings of right and wrong, and an agentic state is when a person is acting because someone else is in authority, rather than acting as an individual. When acting as an individual, a person is in an autonomous state. There is an evolutionary aspect to agency theory. It is likely that humans who worked in a hierarchical social system were more likely to survive. For example, an individual on their own might be more susceptible to predators, so less likely to survive. It is also likely that there is a learned aspect to being in an agentic state, as schools and other social systems rely on power structures and on people obeying those in authority.

*Strengths and weaknesses of agency theory as an explanation for obedience*

| Strengths of agency theory | Weaknesses of agency theory |
|---|---|
| The findings of the variations on Milgram's study back up the theory, because the less they were agents (for example, when the experimenter was not in the room), the less they obeyed. | Social power theory is an alternative explanation. In Milgram's studies the experimenter had reward power, legitimate power and expert power, so could have been obeyed because of being powerful. |

| Strengths of agency theory | Weaknesses of agency theory |
|---|---|
| The theory helps to explain real-life situations such as the Holocaust, where obedience was well beyond what would be expected of autonomous human beings. | The theory is more a description than an explanation. Obedience is defined as obeying an authority figure, so saying that people obey because they are agents of an authority figure does not add much. |

# Study of obedience in a country other than the USA

Here you have a choice of study, but Meeus and Raaijmakers (1986) is suggested for your course and is the chosen study here. This is a study that took place in the Netherlands and is sometimes referred to here as the Dutch study.

## Aim

The aim of Meeus and Raaijmakers was to make the situation more real by using psychological violence. They wanted their participants to believe that they were doing definite harm to the victim. Their study used the kind of violence that might be found in Western societies. They also carried out a second study with the aim of seeing if two variations would reduce obedience, as Milgram's variations did. The two variations were:

- a study with the experimenter absent
- a study with two peer-confederates present, i.e. three people administering the punishment

## General procedure

Meeus and Raaijmakers used a university researcher, the participant and someone applying for a job, so there were three people, as in Milgram's study. The applicant was a trained accomplice who had come to the laboratory to take a test — if he 'passes' the test, he gets the job. The participant had to interrupt the applicant by making 'stress remarks' — negative remarks about the applicant's performance and personality. Participants were told that being able to work under pressure was a requirement of the job for which the applicant was applying. They were also told that the procedure was to help the experimenter's research into the relationship between psychological stress and test achievement. The applicant objected to the interruptions. The participants were told to ignore these objections, which increased as the procedure continued. Due to the stress remarks, the applicant 'failed' the test and 'did not get the job'. The dilemma here for the participant is whether scientific research should affect someone's job and career. The question is whether the participants will cooperate. There were two studies, one is the main study; the other uses the two variations.

### *Procedure for Experiment 1*

| |
|---|
| 39 participants, aged 18–55 years, both males and females, at least Dutch high school education. |
| Volunteer sample through newspaper advertisements, paid a small amount, 24 in an experimental group and 15 in a control group. |

| |
|---|
| Experiment was in a modern building, university campus, male experimenter about 30 years old, well dressed, and friendly though stern. |
| The 'applicant' took a test consisting of 32 multiple-choice questions read out to him — the applicant in a different room listening via a speaker. |
| The participant thought that the applicant was doing a real test for a real job. |
| The participant had to give 15 negative remarks during the test; a TV screen told him/her when to make the remarks and what to say. |
| Electrodes on the applicant's skull measured tension, which was displayed numerically for the participant to see, and he/she was also told verbally about the applicant's stress levels (e.g. 'normal' or 'intense'). |
| The participant heard the applicant ask whether cooperating with the study would affect test performance; the applicant was told it would not, so the participant believed the applicant was lied to. |
| If the participant refused to continue there were four verbal prods, just as in Milgram's study. |

*Procedure for Experiment 2*

| |
|---|
| 41 participants, 22 in the 'experimenter absent' condition and 19 in the 'two peers rebel' condition. |
| The 'experimenter absent' condition was when the experimenter set up the study, ordered the stress remarks and then left the room. |
| The 'two peers rebel' condition was when the real participant was with two other 'participants', although they were really confederates. After stress remark 8 out of 15 both confederates started protesting. After stress remark 10 both confederates stopped making the remarks and the participant was asked to continue. |

## Results of Experiment 1

91.7% of the participants were obedient and made all the stress remarks. 22 of the 24 participants obeyed to the end. None of those in the control group made the stress remarks. Participants discussed whether to continue or not with the experimenter but obeyed without much protest. Follow-up procedures showed participants were upset by the study, 73% believed in the experiment and 45% blamed the experimenter.

## Results of Experiment 2

Obedience was lower in both the situations compared with Experiment 1. 36.4% were fully obedient (made all the stress remarks) in the 'experimenter absent' condition while 15.8% were fully obedient in the 'two peers rebel' condition. For both conditions just over 80% believed in the study.

## Conclusions

Clearly the Dutch study found obedience, as did Milgram, and in fact obedience was much higher. And as with Milgram, the two variations showed lower levels of obedience. So the study supports Milgram's conclusions, and even in a different culture and at a different time high obedience was found, even though participants found obeying distressing. In Experiment 1 about half the participants blamed the experimenter, as if they were agents of the experimenter rather than acting autonomously, which is support for agency theory.

*Strengths and weaknesses of the study by Meeus and Raaijmakers (1986)*

| Strengths | Weaknesses |
|---|---|
| • Deliberately planned so that comparisons could be made with Milgram's studies, which means the results are more interesting and useful | • The situation is not valid, in that the applicant is in a laboratory taking a test for a job, which is not a natural situation |
| • The controls and careful planning mean that the study is replicable and can be tested for reliability and cause-and-effect conclusions are more easily made | • There are differences between the Milgram and Dutch studies, not only the planned differences (e.g. the studies are in different cultures and 20 years apart) |

**Exam preparation** Make sure you can describe and evaluate either the Meeus and Raaijmakers study or another study from a country other than the USA. Prepare the aim, and also prepare for around 6 marks for the procedure, about 4 marks for the results, and about 4 marks for conclusions. Then make sure you can answer a question about evaluating the study.

## Drawing cross-cultural conclusions about obedience

Compare Milgram's main study and one of his variations with Meeus and Raaijmakers's study, including considering whether differences in culture affected differences in findings.

*Comparing Milgram's work with Meeus and Raaijmakers*

| Issue | Comparison point |
|---|---|
| Type of punishment | Milgram asked for physical punishment to be administered (but pretend) and the Dutch study asked for psychological punishment (in more ways real, but still set up). |
| Obedience level for main study | The Dutch study found a much higher level of full obedience. Milgram found 65% whereas Meeus and Raaijmakers found 91.7%. |
| Obedience level with two peers present | Milgram found 10% obeyed in this condition, compared with 15.8% when there was psychological punishment in the Dutch study. |
| Obedience when experimenter was absent | Milgram found 22.5% obedience and the Dutch study found 36.4%. |
| General comparison of obedience levels | The Dutch study found a higher level of obedience in all three conditions. This could be because of the different type of punishment, the different country or the different time (1986 instead of 1963). |

| Issue | Comparison point |
|---|---|
| Effect of different type of punishment | The 'shocks' were less remote than the psychological punishment. For example, Milgram's participants heard screams and felt a slight shock too. |
| Other differences between the two studies | In the Dutch study the participants had agreed to harm the participants, but Milgram's participants had not agreed. So in the Dutch study the participants might have felt they should continue because they had agreed to. Consent levels were different. |
| Agency theory | Both studies support the idea of agency theory because in both cases although the participants were clearly distressed when taking part they continued. It seems that this was not autonomous decision-making. Participants were less obedient without the experimenter there, which suggests that at least in part they were acting as an agent of the experimenter. |

It is hard to show that the greater obedience in the Dutch study was because of it being in a different country, because there were other differences too. It is possible that either a different culture or a different time in history affected the findings, but to find this out a study would have to be perfectly replicated, and Meeus and Raaijmakers made important changes to Milgram's study. Meeus and Raaijmakers conclude that there is still high obedience to authority more than 20 years after Milgram and in a different situation. This suggests that it is not culture that gives obedience or norms of a society, but that obedience is something that would be found in any culture at any time. Perhaps this supports the evolutionary element of agency theory. Note, though, that the Netherlands and the USA are not completely different cultures.

## Ethical issues arising from obedience studies

You need to know about ethical issues in psychology, including those arising from obedience studies. There are five main ethical issues in your course.

### Consent
- Milgram's participants gave consent to a study about learning, but not for a study about obedience and not to give what they thought were strong electric shocks to someone else. So the consent was not informed.
- Meeus and Raaijmakers (1986) obtained consent and informed participants what they were going to be doing, so in that way the Dutch study was more ethical. However, there was some deception, as explained below, so there was some limit to the informed nature of the consent.

### Deceit
- Milgram deceived his participants in a number of ways. They thought the study was about learning, whereas it was about obedience. They thought that the person receiving the 'shocks' was a participant too, though he was really an accomplice. They thought that the 'shocks' were real.

- Meeus and Raaijmakers gave more information to their participants, but there was deceit because the participants thought the job applicant was really applying for a job that would affect his future, whereas the job applicant was a confederate. The responses to the stress remarks were set up too, which was also deceit.

### Right to withdraw
- Milgram took away some of his participants' right to withdraw, because he used four different verbal prods to keep the participant obeying. When the participant objected, he did not immediately let them withdraw from the study. To an extent participants did have the right to withdraw, and indeed some participants did withdraw from the study. After the fourth verbal prod, if the participant still objected, the study was ended.
- Meeus and Raaijmakers also used verbal prods — four as well, to replicate Milgram's study — so they too took away the right to withdraw immediately. Again, to an extent there was a right to withdraw after the fourth verbal prod, as with Milgram's study.

### Competence
- Milgram was competent to carry out the study. He also asked the opinion of colleagues about the study, which increased the level of competence.
- Meeus and Raaijmakers were also competent in terms of where they worked and their experience. They also used Milgram's experiences to learn from.

### Debrief
- Milgram fully debriefed the participants and introduced them to their 'victim', to show that all was well. He set up interviews so that there was support for the participants. Many of them said they were happy to have taken part.
- Meeus and Raaijmakers also fully debriefed their participants. They were fully informed about the study. The researchers do not say any more about ethics, but it has to be assumed that this debrief was thorough and that support was offered.

### Other ethical issues with the studies
- The participants were paid in both studies, which is unethical as it means there is a contract, which the participants may not feel able to break even though they clearly want to. However, at least they were rewarded.
- There was initially confidentiality and the names of the participants were not published.
- The participants were volunteers recruited through newspaper advertisements (for both Milgram's study and the Dutch study), and this seems more ethical as they chose to take part.
- If a participant became distressed, as one did in Milgram's study, observers stepped in to stop the study, which helped to make the study ethical.
- Milgram consulted other people and it was not thought that they would find such a high level of obedience, so he did not intend the study to be as stressful for the participants as it was. Meeus and Raaijmakers, however, knew that the participants would obey (or at least would have had strong reasons to think that there would be high obedience), so perhaps their study was more unethical.

- Ethical guidelines were not as strong in 1963 as they were in 1986, or as they are today, so it is hard to judge the studies by current ethical guidelines. However, it is still useful to do so when considering whether the study was ethical or not.

### Ethical issues because of useful applications

It could be argued that a study should be carried out if the findings can be useful in making society 'better' for people. Milgram's study found that people obey an authority figure to a high level of obedience and that people act as agents of others. The Dutch study found an even higher level of obedience. Knowing this, when people in authority give orders, they now know that others will act as their agents and that they have responsibility for the orders they give. The key issue picks up this idea.

> **Exam preparation** Write an essay on ethical issues in studies of obedience, making sure that you can make at least six points showing that studies are unethical and six points showing how they are ethical.

## Prejudice

As well as obedience you need to know something about prejudice, another area studied within social psychology. You need to know what prejudice is, what discrimination is, and about the social identity theory of prejudice.

### Definitions

- Prejudice is an attitude that is usually negative and means prejudging someone without knowing them. Prejudice is when a judgement is made about someone based on some characteristic (such as race, gender or occupation). Usually it is taken to mean making a negative judgement.
- Discrimination is when action is taken due to prejudice.

### Tajfel's social identity theory as an explanation of prejudice

Social identity theory (SIT) is just one theory of prejudice. The theory suggests that prejudice arises simply from there being two groups. The idea is that our in-group, which is the group we belong to, gives us our self-esteem and identity. To enhance our self-esteem we tend to see those in other groups (the out-groups) negatively — we are prejudiced against them. According to the theory, each of us has several 'selves' according to the different groups we belong to. Our social identity comes from belonging to groups, which means we categorise ourselves as being a member of an in-group. This leads to in-group favouritism and hostility towards the out-group.

Social categorisation is seeing oneself as part of a group. Social identification is identifying with the group. Social comparison is comparing oneself with members of the out-group. As a person's self-concept is wrapped up in the group they will enhance their self-esteem by seeing their group as better than the out-group.

> **Exam preparation** For the social approach you need to be able to define certain terms. These terms include in-group, out-group, social categorisation, social

identification, and social comparison. Make sure you can say what is meant by each of these terms and include an example to help with your definition.

***Strengths and weaknesses of social identity theory as an explanation of prejudice***

| Strengths of social identity theory | Weaknesses of social identity theory |
|---|---|
| There is a lot of evidence to show that people denigrate an out-group and show in-group favouritism. For example, Lalonde (1992) showed how even when members of a team know they are not playing very well they will still unfairly blame another team for their lack of success. | Another theory, realistic conflict theory, suggests that not only must there be two groups but they must be in conflict over resources. Lalonde (1992) studied a hockey team that was competing in a tournament, for example, not 'just' two unconnected groups. |
| The theory is useful and can be applied to real-life situations such as football violence and racial tension. | There are other factors involved in prejudice, not just two groups. For example, in some cases groups co-exist without problems and in others they do not. Prejudice is complex and studies find it hard to capture this complexity, so perhaps findings are not valid. |

**Exam preparation** Be ready to answer a question worth 6 marks for describing social identity theory and 6 marks for evaluating it. This does not mean you would get a question worth 6 marks, but be prepared for that many marks, to give yourself enough material.

# Two studies in detail

You need to know in detail Hofling et al.'s (1966) study of nurses and their obedience to a 'doctor'. You also need to know one other study from three specified on your course. The study chosen here is Reicher and Haslam (2003, 2006). Consider, however, revising the study chosen in your course (which could be Tajfel et al. or Sherif).

## Hofling et al. (1966) study of doctor–nurse relationships

### Aim

Hofling et al. (1966) aimed to study obedience in a real-life situation because they wanted to know more about hospital procedures and they thought there was an issue where a nurse would go against her professional training if asked to by a doctor — someone in higher authority. They wondered how far nurses would obey doctors. Their specific aim was to see if nurses would obey an order they thought came from a doctor, even though by obeying, the nurses would be going against their training.

## Procedure

The study used someone pretending to be a doctor (who was not known to the nurses), who phoned to ask for a dose of a drug to be given to a patient. The procedure was chosen so that the nurses would have to go against their professional training. The nurses should have checked up on the doctor, who was not known to them. The amount was clearly an overdose, as labelled on the bottle. They did not know the drug — it was not on the approved list. Finally, they should not have taken orders over the phone. The study used 22 wards and one nurse from each, thus 22 participants, all female (nurses tended to be female at that time).

Alongside the experiment part of the study, two other groups of nurses completed a questionnaire asking what they would do in the circumstances — the situation was exactly the same as in the field experiment. One group of nurses surveyed consisted of 12 graduate nurses and another group was of 21 student nurses. For the questionnaires, analysis involved checking how many nurses said they would obey, and for the field experiment data were gathered by checking how many nurses actually went to obey. For the field experiment, an observer watched the nurse and the study was stopped when they complied with the order or when they refused — or indeed if the participant was upset or could not find the medication. The observer also interviewed the nurse when they stopped the study, so that there could be debriefing and discussion.

## Results

From the field experiment it was found that 21 of the 22 nurses went to give the medication as ordered. Eleven of the nurses said they did not notice that the amount ordered was an overdose, but they still broke other rules, as outlined above in the procedure. None of the nurses asked for written confirmation, although several asked the doctor to appear promptly. Eighteen of the nurses indicated that they knew they were wrong to obey a telephone order but said this happened often. Sixteen nurses felt they should not have obeyed and some felt guilty or angry. From the questionnaire completed by student nurses it was found that 21 out of 21 said they would not have given the medication and 19 of them noticed the excessive dosage. The questionnaire completed by graduate nurses showed that 10 of the 12 said they would not have given the medication.

## Conclusions

It was clear that in the field experiment there was almost complete obedience, whereas in the surveys there was almost complete lack of obedience. What the nurses said on the questionnaire they would do differed from what they did in reality. Even when they obeyed, it was clear that the nurses knew they were breaking rules, but they said it was done often. The doctor–nurse relationship was strong enough to overcome the nurses' professional training. Hofling et al. concluded that, where there were two intelligences (the trained nurse and the trained doctor), in reality there was only one intelligence, which meant less good patient care. Nurses should be encouraged to use their own training and knowledge. It is a valuable trait that nurses obey doctors, but there is also a potential problem with regard to patient care. The nurses were upset by the study, which prompts questions about the ethics of it, although the aim was to help patients and to improve care, which is an ethically sound aim.

***Strengths and weaknesses of the study by Hofling et al. (1966)***

| Strengths | Weaknesses |
|---|---|
| • The study was carried out in the nurses' natural setting, so there was ecological validity | • There are ethical issues in the study because the nurses were upset that they had been observed and tested without their permission |
| • There were clear controls so the study could be replicated to test for reliability; the results could be said to be because of the situation as set up, rather than other factors | • The study was carried out in 1966, so the findings may not apply in the twenty-first century because doctor–nurse relationships are different |

## Reicher and Haslam (2003, 2006) study of formation of in-groups, focusing on prisoners and guards

### Aims

Reicher and Haslam studied the idea of social identification and they wanted to test it experimentally. Their aim was to find a more ethical and valid way to study such behaviour other than using a laboratory experiment. Their main aim was to investigate tyranny, which they defined as being an unequal system where one group has power (usually oppressive) over another group. A more specific aim was to see if permeability between the two groups (prisoners and guards) would mean no in-group/out-group behaviour, but when the groups were impermeable, then in-groups would form. What they meant by permeability was that people could move between the groups, so when a group is impermeable it is fixed and the people remain in that group.

### Procedure

The researchers worked with the BBC to set up a case study where there was a mock-up prison, prisoners and guards, and observers to see what would happen. The BBC would film the whole experiment (the researchers call it an experimental case study) and some programmes would be broadcast showing the study and what happened. The programmes were broadcast in 2002 and the study has been written up a few times since then. They called their research an experimental case study, as they manipulated variables such as whether a group was impermeable or permeable.

Some 332 participants answered an advertisement and volunteered to take part, and after thorough screening processes and assessment, 27 men were chosen. They were all men because it was easier to provide facilities for one gender and they were all chosen because they were well-adjusted and prosocial, as a baseline measure. For example, if the study found aggression, it could be shown that this aggression came from the study. From the 27, 15 were chosen in order to have a spread of age, class and race. The 15 were matched into five groups of three, and from each of these five groups a guard was chosen randomly, leaving 10 prisoners.

Many sources of data were gathered. Video recordings and tape recordings came from the BBC work. The researchers also measured cortisol levels to check for stress, and they carried out tests to look at issues such as depression, compliance and authoritarianism (how right-wing the prisoners were, for example). The guards were told what to do to an extent — they had to carry out a roll call, allocate work duties and ensure that the prison ran smoothly. The prisoners were not given any instructions.

Permeability was set up by promoting a prisoner after three days and making sure the prisoners knew from the first day that this would happen. Impermeability was set up by having no other promotions and letting the participants know this. The researchers also studied cognitive alternatives — different ways of thinking about a situation — and to do this they introduced one of the prisoners later (so only nine were there at the start). This late entry would bring in new ideas.

### Ethics of the study

The researchers took great care over the ethics of the study. They set up a group of five people as an ethics committee to oversee the study and they also discussed the procedure with colleagues, so there was competence. Participants went through a thorough screening and were told all about the study, so there was informed consent to a large extent. The participants were told they could become stressed and there were two clinical psychologists on hand to monitor individuals. They could ask for a participant to be withdrawn at any time.

### Results

In general, the guards failed to identify together as a group, and so did the prisoners for the first 3 days. But after the groups became impermeable (fixed), the prisoners did set up rules and norms and formed an in-group. The prisoners saw that the guards had not formed a group and eventually became stronger than the guards, thus overthrowing the structure. By day 6 the prisoners broke out of their cells and took over the guards' quarters. Then the whole group decided to run the prison as a commune, but after a few days this did not work, so the group chose strict rules instead. This was against the rules of the study, so it was stopped at that stage.

### Conclusions

The researchers found that groups are formed because of shared norms and values. But when the groups fail, people agree to accept a strong social order even if this goes against their own values. So it is not that tyranny develops because of group behaviour and groups forming, but that tyranny develops when groups fail (the opposite). The study supports social identity theory because it showed that in-groups develop with their own norms and values, and group members categorise themselves in groups and identify with the group. However, the guards did not form a group — it was thought that this was because they did not want to be seen as authoritarian, since that is against social norms and they would be seen on television. This suggests that making behaviour visible may prevent tyranny. It was also found that the guards, who did not form a strong group, showed more mental health problems because of the study, which suggests that mental state is affected by how well groups work.

*Strengths and weaknesses of Reicher and Haslam (2006)*

| Strengths | Weaknesses |
|---|---|
| • The study used multiple methods of collecting the data, so the data could be compared for reliability (if the same results were found by different means) and validity (if the same results were found it is more likely that behaviour was 'real life') | • It was difficult to claim that the interventions caused the behaviour — for example, the prisoners may not have gained a group identity because of the impermeability of the groups but because of other factors, such as not knowing what would happen next; the researchers acknowledge this weakness |
| • The study was set up to adhere to ethical guidelines — for example, with regard to competence, two ethical committees were consulted and one was especially set up for the duration of the study | • The study was televised, which probably affected the behaviour; this could be seen as a strength, because in society people are observed; however, it could be what led to the behaviour, rather than the situation itself |

**Exam preparation** Make sure you know enough for both of your chosen studies to describe each of them for 6 marks, to evaluate them for 6 marks and also to compare them. Consider comparing the aims, the procedures, the research methods, the results and the conclusions separately. You may be asked to compare the studies, and in any case when you can compare them you will know them thoroughly.

# One key issue

You need to know one key issue that can be explained using concepts and ideas from the approach, and you also need to be ready to explain an issue that you are given in the examination. Therefore, you need to be able to use what you have learned for the social approach to explain real-life issues. One issue is explained here, and more issues are given as examples in the exam questions section to help you.

## Blind obedience to authority in a prison setting — Abu Ghraib

The Abu Ghraib prison is in Iraq and was used by the Iraqi government as a prison for many years. When the Iraqi government was removed from power, the prison was used for Iraqi detainees who were guarded by soldiers from the USA. In April 2004 newspapers were filled with photographs and descriptions of the torture of the Iraqi detainees and there was public condemnation of what was clearly unacceptable treatment of them. When people obey orders against their own moral code, this is seen as blind obedience, and it was assumed that the actions of the US soldiers which dehumanised the Iraqis were against their own moral code. The issue here is: why would the soldiers carry out these acts? Was it blind obedience to authority? Should the soldiers be charged with unlawful acts? Were the soldiers being brutal rather than 'just' obeying orders?

> **Exam preparation** Make sure you understand the issue as well as the explanation. Prepare enough to answer a question for about 4 marks on the issue itself. Form the issue into a question so that you are clearly presenting something that needs explaining, as that is what an issue is.

Social psychology can help to explain the brutality in the Abu Ghraib prison in 2004. Milgram's study showed that 65% of the participants gave 'electric shocks' to someone else because they were told to by someone in authority, which suggests that the soldiers would obey orders to torture their Iraqi prisoners because they would be obeying an authority figure. Milgram's participants were very distressed by what they were doing but they still continued. This suggests that the US soldiers would continue to obey orders even though this went against their own moral code and caused moral strain.

Haney et al. carried out a study where participants were allocated to be prisoners or guards and then ran a mock prison. They found that the guards were brutal towards the prisoners — so much so that the study had to be stopped early. This also suggests that the US soldiers would act as guards if put in that role, and it was thought that the situation itself in the Haney et al. study led to the brutality. Zimbardo, who ran the prison in the Haney et al. study, appeared in court as a witness to explain the Abu Ghraib obedience, because he believes that a situation can lead to brutality — that it was not the fault of the soldiers.

Reicher and Haslam found that when groups do not form successfully a situation can lead to tyranny, and this may have occurred in the Abu Ghraib prison. Social identity theory would suggest that when there is a strong in-group, as would be expected among the US soldiers, there is likely to be in-group favouritism and out-group hostility, and this theory could also explain the brutality in the prison.

Hofling et al. (1966) studied how nurses obeyed doctors even when such obedience was against their professional training, which adds to the idea that the US soldiers would obey orders even if it meant very brutal acts. The idea of blind obedience can be explained using agency theory, because soldiers are trained to be agents of authority and agents of society and, as soldiers, they would be agents obeying orders rather than autonomous individuals. These arguments from social psychology all suggest that the US soldiers as individuals were not responsible for their actions, but in law, when such behaviour occurs it is usual for the individual to be blamed.

> **Exam preparation** List concepts from what is given here (e.g. agency theory and social identity theory) and use them to explain another key issue such as football violence. You will find that the concepts and ideas you have studied — such as agency theory, in-group and out-group behaviour, and findings of obedience studies — will be useful in explaining many issues, so learn them ready for the exam in case you are presented with a new issue to explain.

# Practical

You will have carried out at least one practical within social psychology, which will have been either a questionnaire or an interview. Go back over your notes to revise what you did, as it is not possible here to help you to revise that part of the course.

## Some general ideas about the practical and what to learn

Make sure you know about:

- qualitative and quantitative data and how you gathered both types of data
- the aims of your study
- how you drew up either the questionnaire or the interview schedule
- what type of sampling you used and why
- how to use techniques such as Likert-type questions to gather data
- what personal data are and why they are needed
- what is meant by standardised instructions and why they are important
- how to analyse quantitative data in terms of numbers and percentages, for example
- how to analyse qualitative data in terms of generating themes, for example
- ethical issues you addressed, and perhaps any ethical issues you could not address
- issues you controlled, such as how the questions were asked or having the same standardised instructions — and perhaps issues you could not control
- the independent variable, if there was one, such as whether someone was talking about their in-group or out-group or showing how they are agents of someone in authority
- the dependent variable, if there was one, is what was measured to show the concepts being studied (such as a score for preferring in-group members)
- conclusions that you drew, so that you can show that you fully understand what you found

**Exam preparation** Turn the above bullet point list into questions and answer them in preparation. For example, 'What are qualitative and quantitative data? Give an example of each from your own practical.'

# The cognitive approach

Unit 1 covers the social and the cognitive approaches. This section looks at the cognitive approach.

*Summary of the cognitive approach*

**Definition and key terms**

The approach is defined in this section, and key terms are defined where they appear in the Content Guidance section.

> **Methodology**
>
> The main research method you will study within the cognitive approach is the experiment — laboratory, field and natural experiments — together with related terminology. Quite a few of the terms have been covered within the social approach and only the additional terms are explained in this section.
>
> **Content**
>
> Within cognitive psychology — which is a large field — you need to cover the levels of processing theory about memory and one other theory of memory. You also need to know about the cue-dependent theory of forgetting and one other theory of forgetting. Here the 'other' theory of memory chosen is reconstructive memory and the 'other' theory of forgetting is interference theory. Both are chosen because they will be useful for the key issue. If you studied a different 'other' theory for memory and/or forgetting, it is probably best to stick to the one you know.
>
> **Two studies in detail**
>
> You have to cover Godden and Baddeley's (1975) study of divers and whether they forgot more in the same context or when they recalled in a different context. As well as this 'set' study, you have to learn one other from Peterson and Peterson (1959), Craik and Tulving (1975) or Ramponi et al. (2004). Here Craik and Tulving (1975) is chosen because you need it to help you understand the levels of processing framework of how memory works. However, you might like to revise the study that you covered in your own course, if it was a different one.
>
> **One key issue**
>
> You will have studied a key issue in the cognitive approach and could revise that, but here the one chosen is the reliability of eyewitness testimony, so you could use that if you wish (if you studied a different issue).
>
> **Practical**
>
> It is best to use your own practical, as obviously a practical cannot be done here. A list is provided in this section to remind you of what you need to know for the exam.

# Definition and key terms

## Underpinning ideas (assumptions) about the cognitive approach and cognitive psychology

The cognitive approach is about the processing of information. If you think about information coming in through the senses (eyes, ears, nose, mouth and touch), the cognitive approach is about what happens to the information then, including how it is processed in the brain and what the result of that processing is. The multi-store model is a theory of memory that shows clearly one idea of how information is processed in order to retain it (memory), and this model is an example of information processing. There is input, some processing occurs, and then there is output.

*The multi-store model*

The cognitive approach has also used the idea of the brain being like a computer — which has input, processing and output. Using the computer analogy (which is what comparing the brain to a computer is called), ideas can be suggested for how processing (in the form of perceiving, remembering, using language and forgetting) takes place. A model of memory called spreading activation was developed in part to try to understand how to programme a computer to understand language, for example.

## Defining the terms

Terms that you need to be able to define for the cognitive approach are listed. A question will often ask 'What is meant by...' and give the term. The terms are: **information processing, memory, storage, retrieval and forgetting**. In this section on cognitive psychology you will find these terms defined: for example, information processing has already been explained.

> **Exam preparation** Use the idea of information processing and the idea of a computer analogy as two underpinning ideas within cognitive psychology and learn enough to explain both of them for about 4 marks each. Include an example to show your understanding. Then list the five terms given here, and when you have revised the cognitive approach make sure you can say what is meant by each of them (for about 2 or 3 marks, remembering to give an example to show understanding).

# Methodology

What is explained here includes only what you need for the cognitive approach, in addition to what has already been explained within the social approach in the methodology section. First, it is worth considering what you might be asked about regarding the cognitive approach covered earlier in this book. The following table lists what you should already know from having revised the social approach.

### Cognitive approach as covered in this book

| Feature of experiments | Tick if understood |
|---|---|
| Alternative hypothesis | |
| Independent variable (IV) | |
| Dependent variable (DV) | |
| Operationalisation | |
| Control | |
| Situational variables | |
| Participant variables | |
| Condition | |
| Objectivity/subjectivity | |
| Reliability | |
| Validity | |
| Experimenter effects | |
| Demand characteristics | |

**Exam preparation** Check that you understand all the above terms by giving an example for each, whether from a study you have looked at or from an idea for a study of your own.

There are other features of experiments that you need to know about. They are explained here.

## Three types of experiment

There are three types of experiment — laboratory, field and natural experiments. It is rare to come across a natural experiment, but you will study both field and laboratory experiments and you need to know what a natural experiment is.

### Laboratory experiments

- These are experiments carried out in an artificial controlled setting, such as a laboratory. The main feature is control and the setting is an unnatural one for the participants because of this control.
- The independent variable (IV) is manipulated in some way, usually using two conditions, sometimes more. For example, some participants could be asked to learn and recall a list of words that all had a similar theme. Another group of participants could be asked to learn and recall a list with the same number of words, of similar length, but this time a random list without a theme. There would be two conditions — whether the list had words with a theme (such as all colour words) or no theme (randomly chosen). The IV is whether words have a theme or not.

- The dependent variable (DV) is recorded, and in the example here the DV would be how many of the words in the list were recalled by each participant.
- Participant and situational variables would be controlled in a laboratory experiment, for example by using the same room at the same time of day (situational variables) and making sure as far as possible that participants were not hungry in one of the conditions and not the other, and so on (participant variables).
- The aim of a laboratory experiment is to find a cause and effect conclusion so that scientific knowledge can be built.

## Field experiments

These are experiments carried out 'in the field', which means in the participants' natural setting. This can be, for example, a school, for teachers or pupils, a hospital, for doctors, nurses or patients, or a prison, for prisoners and guards. The main feature is the natural setting, together with the controls of a laboratory experiment, though these may be difficult to put into place.

Apart from the natural setting, field experiments have the same features as laboratory experiments, including IV, DV, controls and aiming for cause-and-effect conclusions.

## Natural experiments

- These are experiments that tend to be 'in the field' because the independent variable occurs naturally. This is the main feature — that the IV is not something manipulated or set up, but is found already 'out there'.
- For example, when researchers wanted to see the effects of television on children they studied a community where television was to be introduced. They studied the community beforehand and afterwards, and those were the two conditions of the IV. They did not introduce the television; it was being introduced in any case — it was a naturally occurring situation.
- Other independent variables (not only those in a natural setting) can be naturally occurring, such as gender. However, usually experiments using this sort of naturally occurring IV (such as gender rather than something in the natural setting) are called quasi-experiments because in other respects they are like laboratory experiments and can take place in a laboratory. Truly natural experiments tend to be 'in the field' and have a more complex IV (for example, the introduction of television is more complex than someone's gender).

### Strengths of the different types of experiment

| Laboratory | Field | Natural |
|---|---|---|
| Good controls; replicable; reliability can be tested | More ecologically valid than laboratory experiments because they take place in natural settings | Independent variable occurs naturally, so valid because not artificially set up |
| Good controls; cause-and-effect relationship can be established | Fairly replicable because of experimental features | Tend to take place in a natural environment so likely to be ecologically valid |

*Weaknesses of the different types of experiment*

| Laboratory | Field | Natural |
|---|---|---|
| So controlled that tasks may not give valid results because they are not natural/real | Natural setting, so hard to control all factors, which means results may be less valid | Difficult to control variables because the independent variable is naturally occurring, making it difficult to isolate all factors that might affect results |
| Environment unnatural and controlled, so not ecologically valid | Hard to control because of natural setting, so may not be replicable | Hard to control for experimenter effects; using a double-blind technique is not straightforward because most are carried out in natural settings |
| Experimenter effects can mean results are not valid because there may then be bias | Experimenter effects can mean results are not valid because there may then be bias | |

## Experimental (participant) designs

There are three **experimental designs**, sometimes called **participant designs** to remind you that they concern the participants in an experiment. There are only three ways of sorting participants into groups to study them.

- **Independent groups design** means to have different participants for each condition. Each group is independent of the other groups with regard to the people doing the study. If one group learns and recalls words that have colour meaning and a different group learns and recalls random words, this is an independent groups design.
- **Repeated measures design** means that all the conditions involve the same participants. For example, the person who learns and recalls the words that have colour meaning is also the person who learns and recalls the random words.
- **Matched pairs design** means different participants in the conditions, as in an independent groups design. But the participants are matched so that the two groups have 'as if' the same people. For example, if one participant is male, aged 20 and a student, there will be another 20-year-old male student in the other group.

*Strengths of the different participant designs*

| Repeated measures | Independent groups | Matched pairs |
|---|---|---|
| Participant variables are controlled because all participants do all conditions | No order effects to affect results | Helps to control participant variables |
| Uses fewer participants, so more efficient in terms of cost, convenience and ethics | Demand characteristics less likely | No order effects |

**Weaknesses of the different participant designs**

| Repeated measures | Independent groups | Matched pairs |
|---|---|---|
| Order effects such as practice and fatigue effects can affect the results if there is no counter-balancing | Participant variables may affect the results | Different people are used, so there may be participant variables that affect the results |
| Demand characteristics are possible because participants could guess the aim(s) of the study | More participants are needed, so less efficient and less ethical | More participants are needed, so less efficient in terms of cost and less ethical |

## Experimental hypothesis (and whether directional or non-directional)

- In most studies there is a hypothesis (though there are exceptions, as in case studies, which you will study later in your course).
- A hypothesis is a statement of what is expected. So in the example that has been used in this section it could be said that the hypothesis is 'It is expected that more words from a list of words with colour meaning are going to be recalled than words from a list where the words are random.'
- There is a **null hypothesis**, which is the one that is tested, and which you will learn more about in Unit 2. The null hypothesis is that there is no difference as predicted (e.g. no difference in recall for the two lists).
- There is the **alternative hypothesis** — the alternative to the null — that there is a difference as predicted.
- In an experiment, the alternative is the **experimental hypothesis**.

Hypotheses (predictions) can be directional or non-directional.
- A **directional hypothesis** means that the direction of the difference is predicted. So if a hypothesis says that the words from the 'colour words' list are better remembered than the words from the 'random' list, this is directional (one list is *better* remembered).
- A **non-directional hypothesis** is where the direction is not predicted. For example, if the experimental hypothesis is that there is a difference in the number of words recalled depending on whether a list is of 'colour' words or a list of random words, this does not give the direction.
- If we say boys are more aggressive than girls, we give direction (directional). If we say children differ in aggression according to gender, we don't give direction (non-directional).
- For information, because you will need to know in Unit 2 and also because of the way the questions might be asked, 'directional' is sometimes called 'one-tailed' and 'non-directional' is sometimes called 'two-tailed'.

## Order effects, counterbalancing and randomisation

If different people are doing the different conditions (conditions are the parts of the study, e.g. there are words with colour meaning to learn and there are words of random meaning to learn — two conditions), they won't learn from doing one condition and so do another one better. In addition, they won't get tired and do a second condition worse. However, if the same people do all the conditions they may well get practised and get better, or get tired and get worse. These two situations are called **order effects**, as they are due to the order in which the conditions are carried out. If a participant does worse because he or she becomes tired, this is called a **fatigue effect**. If a participant does better because they are more practised, this is called a **practice effect**.

There are two ways of avoiding order effects. One is to **counterbalance**, which means alternating the order in which the participant does the conditions. The other way is called **randomisation**, which means choosing the order in which the participant does the conditions, for example by tossing a coin.

*Order effects and how to deal with them*

| Order effect/issue | What it means |
|---|---|
| Practice effect | Having done one of the tasks (conditions), the participant does the next one better because of having had practice. |
| Fatigue effect | Having done one of the tasks (conditions), the participant does the next one less well because of being tired. |
| Counterbalancing | Alternating the order in which the tasks are presented, to counteract order effects. If the first participant does task A then task B, the next does task B then task A. There would perhaps still be order effects but they would cancel each other out. |
| Randomisation | Choosing at random which task the participant will do first. This can be done by tossing a coin (e.g. heads it is task A first). |

**Exam preparation** Make sure you can say what is meant by all the terms used in this methodology section, and that you really understand the issues raised. You have to be able to answer questions about stimulus material, so you have to be able to use all the ideas. You could read the two methodology sections (for social and cognitive psychology) together and make your own glossary of terms.

# Content

The content for cognitive psychology that you need to cover is clear: two models or theories of memory and two models or theories of forgetting. Four theories are explained briefly here. Some explanations are called theories, some are called models and one mentioned here is called a framework. It is hard to be precise about the differences between theory, model and framework, but this table gives suggestions about the differences.

*Theory, model and framework*

| Term | 'What is meant by...' |
|---|---|
| Theory | Can be tested and predicts what will happen. A hypothesis is taken from a theory and then tested. If the hypothesis is supported by evidence, the theory continues; if not, it is amended or replaced. |
| Model | Involves generating an abstract idea of how something might happen and is not a theory until it is made testable against reality. |
| Framework | Suggests an idea or thought that is not firmed up enough (yet) to be a model or a theory ready to be tested. |

# Two theories/models of memory

The levels of processing framework and the reconstruction theory of memory are the two explained here. Memory is defined as taking in information that is then available for use later on, and is often said to have three stages — encoding, storage and retrieval. Information has to be encoded, which means memories are laid down in some way, and this is a physical trace in the brain. As well as encoding, the memory has to be stored, otherwise if the trace is lost, the information will have been forgotten. Storage is retaining the memory and keeping it in some way. If we are to remember something, that information has to be retrieved, which means getting the information back when required.

The key terms you need to be able to define for cognitive psychology are **information processing**, **memory**, **storage**, **retrieval and forgetting**. Forgetting is defined later in this section, and information processing (input, processing and output) was explained at the start of the material on cognitive psychology (see page 44). Here memory, storage and retrieval are explained. Make sure you can say what is meant by all five of these terms.

### Levels of processing framework (LOP)

The levels of processing framework is an idea of how memory might occur. Information is processed at different levels, such as deeply attended to or less deeply attended to. Remembering information is about how deeply it is processed, rather than memory being 'something' in itself. According to this framework there are three levels of processing.

*Three levels of processing according to LOP*

| Level | Explanation |
|---|---|
| Structural (sight) | Processing at a structural level is seeing what something is like, e.g. with words, whether there are capital letters or lower case (i.e. TABLE or table), or how many letters go below the line (e.g. 'y', 'g'). |

| Level | Explanation |
|---|---|
| Phonemic (sound) | Processing phonemically means considering how something sounds, e.g. with words, whether one word rhymes with another (e.g. cat, mat) or not (e.g. cat, dog). |
| Semantic (meaning) | Processing semantically means considering the meaning of something, e.g. with words, what the word means. For example, whether a word fits in a sentence (e.g. cat: 'the cat has smooth fur' compared with table: 'the table has smooth fur'). |

According to this framework, memory comes from depth of processing. If there is no depth of processing — such as when no attention at all is paid to something — there is no memory trace. If there is shallow processing — such as structural processing — there is not a strong memory trace. However, if there is deep processing — such as when meaning is considered — there is a stronger memory trace.

Craik and Tulving's (1975) study explains the levels of processing idea and is described in the 'Two studies in detail' on pp. 58–59.

*Strengths and weaknesses of the levels-of-processing framework*

| Strengths | Weaknesses |
|---|---|
| • There is evidence for the framework: Hyde and Jenkins (1971) and Craik and Tulving (1975) | • Depth of processing also tends to mean more time spent processing; it might be that the time spent makes the memory stronger, not the depth of processing |
| • It links research into memory with research into perception and selective attention; it focuses on information processing and the whole process; this means it is a stronger explanation than the multi-store model, because more studies can be explained by it | • There may be more effort involved in 'deeper' processing and the greater effort might account for the better recall; the term 'deep' is not well defined by Craik and Lockhart (1972); it could be time spent processing, effort involved or using past experiences and adding meaning |

## Reconstructive memory

Bartlett was a well-known psychologist working as long ago as 1932 and he developed a theory that is still used and respected today. He made famous the idea that memory is not a completely accurate recording of what happens in life. He put forward the idea that we use our past experiences when recording current events and laying down memories. He said we have schemata (plural of schema) — which are plans and information about things that we have already learned or assumed. For example, you have a schema for eating in a restaurant — you know that you have to order, and that you have to pay at the end, and that you use a knife and fork, and so on. We process information through these schemata without knowing it, and this means our memories are affected and what we recall is not 'pure' information. 'Remembering' is not just playing back a video recording as we would from a mobile phone — it is using what was seen or heard and relating the story which is filtered through past experiences and schemata. This means that memory is reconstructed.

Bartlett (1932) ran a famous experiment to illustrate his theory of reconstruction. He read participants a story called *The War of the Ghosts*, which was a story from a different culture that did not make sense easily, so the participants did not have a schema for all the events in the story. He found a number of features in the recall of the story. He found that participants added to the story so that it made sense to them, which he called confabulation. They altered some important parts to fit their own schemata too, which he called rationalisation. For example, the story ends with someone 'falling down dead' at sunrise, whereas people tended to say it was at sunset as that fitted better for them. He found that participants picked out central features (to them) of the story and missed out other bits — usually what did not make sense to them. And when he asked them to remember it again, after a short while, they recalled less. Using this story, he showed that people reconstructed the story so that it made sense and to fit their schemata.

### Strengths and weaknesses of the theory of reconstructive memory

| Strengths | Weaknesses |
| --- | --- |
| • There is much evidence for the theory: Bartlett (1932) and the work of Loftus on eyewitness testimony | • Bartlett's (1932) story did not make sense so participants may have altered it because of demand characteristics |
| • The theory can be tested experimentally | • The theory describes memory as reconstructive but does not deal with the processes |

**Exam preparation**  Make sure you can clearly describe both the memory theories/models that you have studied and that you can evaluate them both as well. Then create a table comparing the two of them, such as the one started below. This will help you to understand them fully.

### Comparisons between levels of processing and reconstruction theory

| Levels of processing framework | Theory of reconstructive memory |
| --- | --- |
| Used laboratory experiments when testing — using lists of words. | Used experiments when testing — using stories. |
| Suggests memory is not a thing but just part of processing information, and only occurs when information is processed quite deeply. | Suggests memory is something to study on its own, that is part of processing information but not 'just' a by-product of processing as suggested by LOP. |
| Looks at three levels of processing, including using meaning. | Looks at the effects of previous experiences and schemata on recall. |
| Has a useful application in revision and studying as well as in helping recall — it is known that to remember you need to add meaning. | Has a useful application in the legal system because eyewitness testimony can be taken as absolute, but the theory suggests it is not like a tape recording and is affected by previous experience. |

# Two theories/models of forgetting

The cue-dependent and interference theory of forgetting are the two explained here. One point about memory and forgetting is worth taking note of. In your course, when you are writing about forgetting, try to focus on that and not on remembering. For example, when discussing the reconstructive elements of memory you might want to talk about forgetting material that does not 'fit' — but try to focus on memory being altered by schemata and not on what is forgotten. Similarly, with cue-dependent forgetting, you will see that you could talk about cues helping us to remember, but try to focus on lack of cues leading us to forget.

## Cue-dependent forgetting

Cue-dependent forgetting theory was put forward by Tulving (1975), who suggested that the absence of cues leads to forgetting. Tulving defined forgetting as 'the inability to recall something now that could be recalled on an earlier occasion'. Cues are things in the environment that were present when the memory was encoded — and Tulving was talking about the cognitive environment. Such cues are called retrieval cues. The cognitive environment is what is around both externally and internally when memories are encoded, so those features are encoded too, or at least affect encoding. Encoding means laying down memories. Forgetting occurs, according to the cue-dependent theory of forgetting, when the cognitive environment is different from what it was when a memory was encoded. It follows that forgetting is reduced if the cognitive environment is reinstated.

Two types of cue are discussed in the theory of cue-dependent forgetting. There are cues — state-dependent cues — that depend on the emotional state of the individual or their physical state, such as hunger or tiredness. There are cues that depend on the context someone is in — context-dependent cues — such as their actual environment (where they are) and things around them. The theory suggests that there is state-dependent forgetting, because the person is not in the same state as they were when memories were encoded. In addition, there is context-dependent forgetting, which occurs because the person is not in the same situation as when the memories were encoded.

Godden and Baddeley's (1975) field experiment studied cue-dependent forgetting and is explained in the section that follows, looking at two studies in detail. Use evidence from their study to help to describe and evaluate the cue-dependent theory of forgetting.

*Strengths and weaknesses of the cue-dependent theory of forgetting*

| Strengths | Weaknesses |
|---|---|
| • This theory accounts for forgetting in different tasks. There are many supporting studies | • Tasks are artificial, so the results might lack validity |
| • The idea is testable because the retrieval environment can be replicated | • It may only account for some forms of forgetting |

**content guidance**

## The interference theory of forgetting

Interference theory suggests that forgetting occurs because some information interferes with other information. Memory is often split into short-term memory, which lasts up to 30 seconds and holds a limited amount of information, and long-term memory, which potentially lasts a lifetime and holds an unlimited amount of information. In short-term memory, interference causes forgetting when some information prevents other information from being encoded into long-term memory. The interference theory of forgetting also looks at forgetting in long-term memory. The idea is that information already stored in long-term memory can get in the way of encoding and storing new information. Another way that interference causes forgetting is that new information can interfere with what is already stored.

*Two types of interference causing forgetting in long-term memory*

| Type of interference | Explanation | Example |
|---|---|---|
| Retroactive interference | Material that is learned now gets in the way of (interferes with) material that has been previously stored, so retrieval is affected (there is forgetting). | Learning French now gets in the way of previously learned Spanish (you remember the French word but have now forgotten the Spanish word that you knew before). |
| Proactive interference | Material that was learned in the past gets in the way of (interferes with) material that is being stored now, so retrieval is affected (there is forgetting). | Learned Spanish — words you already know — gets in the way of learning French now (you remember the Spanish word but that gets in the way of you remembering the French word). |

*Strengths and weaknesses of the interference theory of forgetting*

| Strengths | Weaknesses |
|---|---|
| • There is much evidence to support the theory, e.g. Jenkins and Dallenbach (1924) | • It is hard to separate interference from displacement and trace decay; it can be shown that interference seems to happen but not why this happens or what occurs |
| • It has been tested by experiment, giving cause-and-effect relationships. Experiments have been replicated and appear to be reliable | • Tasks used in experiments are artificial and may lack validity |

*Comparing two theories of forgetting*

| Cue-dependent theory of forgetting | Interference theory of forgetting |
|---|---|
| Used laboratory experiments to test the theory, which can lack validity because of artificial tasks. | Used laboratory experiments to test the theory, which can lack validity because of artificial tasks. |

| Cue-dependent theory of forgetting | Interference theory of forgetting |
|---|---|
| Considers what was in the environment and how not reproducing that would give forgetting (prevent retrieval). | Considers what is already stored in long-term memory and how that would affect storage of new material. |
| The theory considers how encoding (including cues) affects storage (the theory includes cues and how material is stored), which would affect retrieval. | The theory considers how storage (what was stored) would affect retrieval. |
| Suggests that reinstating the cognitive environment (cues) would help stop forgetting. | Seems to suggest that forgetting is inevitable if material is similar. |

**Exam preparation**   Make sure you can clearly describe both the forgetting theories/models that you have studied and that you can evaluate them both as well. Then create a table comparing the two of them, such as the one started above. This will help you to understand them fully.

# Two studies in detail

The two studies in detail explained here are Godden and Baddeley's (1975) study of divers and how context affects forgetting, and Craik and Tulving's (1975) study of levels of processing. Godden and Baddeley's study helps to describe and evaluate the cue-dependent theory of forgetting, and it is a compulsory study, so you have to know about it. Craik and Tulving's study helps to describe and evaluate the levels of processing framework for explaining memory and it is a choice in your course. If you have studied either Peterson and Peterson (1959) or Ramponi et al. (2004) instead, you could revise that study instead of learning Craik and Tulving.

## Godden and Baddeley's (1975) study of divers

### Aims
Godden and Baddeley wanted to study the effect of environment on recall and the effect of retrieval cues. They aimed to look at context cues rather than state cues. Their specific aim was to see if there was better recall when the recall environment was the same as the learning environment. They chose two natural environments and the two environments were clearly different, so that the contexts were clearly different. They wanted to have a valid study, so they used naturally occurring environments and did a field study.

### Procedure
- Godden and Baddeley chose divers as their participants. There were 13 male and five female participants, who were all members of a diving club. They were on a diving holiday in Scotland.

content guidance

- They chose 'underwater' as one environment and 'on land' as the other environment.
- The same divers had to learn a list of words either on land ('dry') or underwater ('wet'). Then they had to recall the words either on land ('dry') or underwater ('wet'). There were 36 words of two or three syllables, randomly chosen.
- So there were four conditions:
  - 'dry' learning and 'dry' recall
  - 'dry' learning and 'wet' recall
  - 'wet' learning and 'wet' recall
  - 'wet' learning and 'dry' recall
- The first two ('dry' and 'dry' and 'wet' and 'wet') were where the retrieval cues were the same as the cues at encoding and storage.
- The second two ('dry' and 'wet' and 'wet' and 'dry') were where the cues at encoding and storage were not present as retrieval cues for recall.
- The hypothesis was that divers would remember more words (forget less) if the learning and recall environments were the same (either learning and recalling underwater or learning and recalling on land) than if the learning and recall environments were different (either learning underwater and recalling on land or learning on land and recalling underwater).
- The independent variable is whether the two contexts (environments) are the same or different.
- The dependent variable was how many words are correctly recalled.
- The same divers did all four conditions, so this was a repeated measures design.

## Results

### Percentage of words recalled out of 36 words depending on the learning and recall contexts

| Learning environment | Recall environment dry | Recall environment wet |
|---|---|---|
| Dry | 37 | 24 |
| Wet | 23 | 32 |

The table shows that the percentages were higher when the learning environment and the recall environment were the same (37% and 32%). When the learning environment and recall environment were different, recall was lower (23% and 24%).

## Conclusions

Context is a retrieval cue, and when the cognitive environment at recall is the same as at encoding, forgetting is less.

### Strengths and weaknesses of the Godden and Baddeley (1975) study

| Strengths | Weaknesses |
|---|---|
| • It was an experiment with clear controls, so replicable; this means it can be tested for reliability and is a scientific study | • The situation was artificial and the contexts were very different; this means the results may not be valid |
| • The environment was familiar to the participants, who were divers, so there was some ecological validity | • The results showed a lot of forgetting even when the context for encoding and recall were the same; therefore, context dependency cannot be the only reason for forgetting |

# Craik and Tulving's (1975) study of levels of processing

## Aims

The main aim of Craik and Tulving's (1975) study was to test the levels of processing (LOP) framework. They wanted to see if structural processing led to low recall, phonemic processing led to better recall and semantic processing led to the best recall, which is what LOP suggests. When they talked about better recall they meant that the memory trace was durable — it would fade most quickly when material was structurally processed and least quickly with semantic processing. They also wanted to see if semantic processing meant processing for a longer time.

## Procedure

- They operationalised shallow processing by asking participants to consider the structure of words, such as whether the word is in upper or lower case letters.
- They operationalised intermediate processing by asking participants to consider whether a word rhymed with another word or not, which is phonemic processing.
- They operationalised deep processing by asking participants to answer questions based on considering the meaning of a word, which is semantic processing.
- Participants were tested individually. Words were flashed up on a screen in front of the participant after a question had been asked. The questions required either structural processing, phonemic processing or semantic processing. After the word was quickly flashed in front of them, the participant had to press 'yes' or 'no' as their answer. The questions were set up so that the numbers requiring 'yes' and 'no' answers were even.
- All participants did all the questions, so this was a repeated measures design.
- After all the questions had been answered, the participants were given an unexpected recognition or recall task. There were a number of experiments with slightly different procedures, but the procedure given here is the basic one. For example, for one experiment 40 questions were asked, so 40 words were used in the test condition; then the recognition task used 80 words and the participants had to say whether the words had been part of the task or not.

## Results

In one experiment Craik and Tulving asked five different questions which required 'yes' or 'no' responses. The results of asking these five questions, with the proportion of the words correctly recognised and the time it took to reply, are given here.

*Time taken to answer 'yes' or 'no' to the five questions*

| Response time in milliseconds | Level of processing from shallow (1) to deepest (5) | | | | |
|---|---|---|---|---|---|
| | (1) Is there a word? | (2) Is the word in capital letters? | (3) Does the word rhyme? | (4) Does the word fit the category? | (5) Does the word fit the sentence? |
| Yes | 591 | 614 | 689 | 711 | 741 |
| No | 590 | 625 | 678 | 716 | 832 |

It can be seen that the more the question required thinking about (more depth of processing, perhaps), the longer it took for the participant to press either 'yes' or 'no'. This was true both for 'yes' and 'no' answers. It took a little longer to respond to 'no' questions when thinking about whether a word fitted a sentence, but for the other levels, whether the answer was 'yes' or 'no' made little difference to the time.

*Proportion of words recognised correctly for answers 'yes' or 'no' to the five questions*

| Proportion of words recognised correctly | Level of processing from shallow (1) to deepest (5) | | | | |
| --- | --- | --- | --- | --- | --- |
| | (1) Is there a word? | (2) Is the word in capital letters? | (3) Does the word rhyme? | (4) Does the word fit the category? | (5) Does the word fit the sentence? |
| Yes | 0.22 | 0.18 | 0.78 | 0.93 | 0.96 |
| No | N/A | 0.14 | 0.36 | 0.63 | 0.83 |

The first two questions (whether there is a word and whether the word is in capital letters) can both be considered as structural processing, and the last two questions can both be considered as needing semantic processing. Looking at the questions as having three depths (1 + 2, 3, 4 + 5), it is clear that the proportion of words recognised correctly depends on the depth of processing, with structural processing giving the least recognition, graduating to phonemic processing, and semantic processing giving the most recognition. This was the case for both 'yes' and 'no' answers. When a word rhymed, however (a 'yes' answer), there was a much better recognition rate than if the word did not rhyme (a 'no' answer), which you might think is because the meaning of the word was then better recorded.

## Conclusions

Craik and Tulving's study backs up the LOP idea and shows that semantic processing leads to the best recall and also takes longer. It could be that depth of processing leads to better recall, or that length of processing leads to better recall, or some combination of these issues.

*Strengths and weaknesses of the study by Craik and Tulving (1975)*

| Strengths | Weaknesses |
| --- | --- |
| • The experiments were controlled carefully, so the study is replicable; replication occurred within the study so the findings are reliable | • Even if 'deeper' means longer processing, it might still be that the improved recognition is due to the length of processing time, not the depth of processing |
| • The study reinforces the levels-of-processing framework; the study looks at depth meaning longer processing time | • The tasks are artificial, so the study could lack validity |

**Exam preparation** Compare the two studies, because when comparing you really have to understand them and this will help your revision.

*Comparisons between the two studies*

| Godden and Baddeley (1975) | Craik and Tulving (1975) |
|---|---|
| An experimental study carried out in 1975, using careful controls to look for cause and effect links. | An experimental study carried out in 1975 using careful controls to look for cause and effect links. |
| A field experiment that can claim ecological validity to an extent because it used divers in their natural environment. | A laboratory experiment that loses out on ecological validity as the setting was not natural for processing meaning in everyday life. |
| Uses words to test recall, which may not be valid because there is a lot more to memory than learning words. | Uses words to test recall, which may not be valid because there is a lot more to memory than learning words. |
| Gives clear evidence to back the theory of cue-dependent forgetting, showing that the context where learning takes place helps recall. | Gives clear evidence to back the theory of levels of processing, showing that the deeper the processing the better the recall. |

# One key issue

The key issue chosen is whether eyewitness testimony is reliable or not, and what the consequences are if it is unreliable. Eyewitness testimony is the statement given by someone who has seen an accident or crime — usually to the police — to say what they have seen. People can then give evidence in a court to say what they have seen, which is also eyewitness testimony. An eyewitness can be asked to pick someone out of a line-up, help to draw up an identikit picture of someone, or identify them in some other way. The point is that in general, it is thought that an eyewitness will be able to identify a suspect and give a good account of a situation. In practice, however, it seems that eyewitnesses can be unreliable. There are cases where someone has been imprisoned because of eyewitness testimony and then later it has been found that the person was not guilty. The issue is that eyewitness testimony appears to be unreliable.

Cognitive psychology can explain why eyewitness testimony is likely to be unreliable. One explanation is to consider the role of schemata in memory, as proposed by Bartlett (1932). Bartlett suggested that memory is not like a tape recorder, but instead involves amending material to ensure it makes sense and fits our schemata. There is likely to be confabulation, where someone will add to memory so that it makes sense. There is also rationalisation, which means features will be forgotten, again to make sense of what the eyewitness has seen.

Elizabeth Loftus carried out many studies on the unreliability of eyewitness testimony, including a study by Loftus and Palmer (1975), which showed that, when a verb in a question was changed, it affected the response to a question. When Loftus and Palmer asked about the speed of a car that 'smashed', 'hit', or 'collided with' (and other verbs) another car, the estimate of speed was higher for 'smashed' — presumably because it suggests the car was going faster. This suggests that leading questions guide eyewitness testimony. Another study showed that if an eyewitness was asked about 'a' broken headlight, there was less recall of broken glass than if they were asked about 'the' broken headlight, again showing the strength of leading questions.

On the other hand, Loftus also found later that only fairly unimportant information is affected by such leading questions — very important information seems less affected by how a question is worded. Nevertheless, Loftus found that if participants in a study were told there was an eyewitness to an incident, they were much more likely to believe the eyewitness, even if without that testimony there was not enough evidence for them to be so confident. It seems that juries believe eyewitnesses, even though their testimony is likely to be unreliable. Loftus and Ketcham (1991) suggested that eyewitness testimony might be responsible for an incorrect verdict about half of the time.

**Exam preparation** Be ready for an issue that you will be given in the exam, to which you have to apply concepts from the approach. One idea might be the issue of helping someone to revise for an exam (focus on depth of processing or reinstating the context or state). Another idea is considering how to get more accurate eyewitness testimony from a witness (avoid leading questions or allow them to recall without guiding them to how to do this). Practise using the ideas you have learned from cognitive psychology to explain such issues.

# Practical

You will have carried out at least one practical within cognitive psychology, which will have been an experiment. Go back over your notes to revise what you did, as it is not possible here to help you to revise that part of the course.

## Some general ideas about the practical and what to learn

Make sure you know about:
- the aim(s) of the practical
- the purpose of using the type of experiment you used (e.g. laboratory, field)
- your experimental hypothesis and null hypothesis
- the independent and dependent variable (fully operationalised)
- whether the hypothesis is directional or non-directional
- the participant design and why you chose that design
- the sampling method, why you chose it, and what other method you might have chosen
- ethical issues and how they were dealt with
- ethical issues, which should have been dealt with more fully
- the apparatus and why you chose it (e.g. why you chose those words, if applicable)

- whether you used counterbalancing and what you did about order effects (if you used repeated measures)
- what controls you put into place and why — and what was not controlled
- two problems with your study, apart from ethical issues and controls
- possible issues with regard to experimenter effects
- strengths of your study — considering issues such as validity, reliability, generalisability, objectivity and credibility
- which descriptive statistics you used (mean, median, mode, range, graphs) and why
- what the range means and why it is important
- how to draw and interpret a frequency graph

**Exam preparation** Practise using the above bullet points as questions and prepare answers (such as which design you chose and why).

# Questions
# &
# Answers

- Questions are presented in two sections, one for each of the two approaches. The separate sections will help you to revise and practise questions.
- Remember: the paper will not split the questions up by approach, so expect either of the approaches for any question. Expect the paper to ask about any of the six areas within each approach at any time.
- To remind you, the two approaches are the social approach and the cognitive approach. The six areas are the definitions, methodology, content, studies in detail, key issue and practical.
- Choose one approach and revise the material using this unit guide. Work through the questions for your chosen approach, answering them yourself without reading the advice on how to answer the question and without reading the answer given.
- Then mark your own answers, and read through the advice on what is required. Did you interpret the question successfully? Read through the answers given and note where the marks are awarded. Finally, read through the examiner's comments to see what a full answer should include.
- Once you have prepared answers for all the questions in a particular approach, answer them again but this time choose a different topic. For example, if you answered a question on one study in detail, answer it again using the other study in detail that you have prepared. If you have described a theory of memory within the cognitive approach, describe your other chosen theory of memory. If the question is about one in-depth area (e.g. obedience), answer it as if it were about the other in-depth area (e.g. prejudice). In this way you are making up your own questions, which is useful preparation for the examination.
- There is a paper that you can work through, with a mark scheme, in the sample assessment materials prepared for your course. You can find that paper on the Edexcel website (www.edexcel.org.uk), so work through that as well.

## Examiner's comments

All questions and answers are followed by examiner's comments. These are preceded by the icon *e*. They indicate where credit is due and point out areas for improvement, specific problems and common errors such as poor time management, lack of clarity, weak or non-existent development, irrelevance, misinterpretation of the question and mistaken meanings of terms.

# S\ection 1

# The social approach

## Definitions

**(1) In the boxes below, tick the two statements that apply to the social approach.** (2 marks, AO1)

(a) Individuals cannot be understood outside their culture ☐

(b) Interactions between people are important ☐

(c) Information is processed by the brain; there is input, processing and output ☐

(d) An individual is governed most by their biological structure ☐

🖉 This is a multiple-choice question with two right answers. Read all the statements carefully. First, identify those you think are right, and second, quickly check that the other two statements are definitely wrong. Then you can be sure you are ticking the right boxes.

### Answer

(a) Individuals cannot be understood outside their culture ✔ ✓

(b) Interactions between people are important ✔ ✓

(c) Information is processed by the brain; there is input, processing and output ☐

(d) An individual is governed most by their biological structure ☐

🖉 Information processing refers to cognitive processing, and the social approach does not look at biological factors, so only the first two can be right.

**(2) Describe what is meant by social psychology.** (4 marks, AO1)

🖉 This question is more likely to ask what is meant by the social approach, but get used to seeing the question asked in different ways. This is about the definition of the approach. Think about any assumptions underlying the approach. It would be useful to give an example to show understanding, but the example must be fully explained, not just mentioned.

### Answer

Social psychology looks at people as groups and how they behave in groups. ✓ For example, social identity theory suggests that self-esteem is to do with identifying with a group, and this means in-group favouritism and out-group hostility, which explains prejudice. ✓ Social psychology looks at people as social beings, including issues such as why some individuals obey others even when it goes against their own moral code. Social psychology focuses on an individual, but more on how an individual fits in with others within a society than on the individual themselves. ✓ There is a focus on inter-actions between people; issues such as crowd behaviour, helping others, prejudice and obedience are examples of topics covered. ✓

e This answer relies on examples quite a lot, but that is fine because they are clearly explained to show underlying principles of the approach, such as the focus on groups and interactions between individuals. If you are using an example, make sure you either give quite a few instances, as in the last point, or you explain fully, as in the second point.

**(3) Explain what is meant by agentic state and in-group behaviour. In your answer give an example of each.**    (6 marks, AO1)

e Assume there are 3 marks for each term, and that in each case 1 of those marks is for the example. The other 2 marks in each case will be given for a clear definition, and a weaker definition will get 1 mark.

## Answer

The agentic state is a term used in Milgram's agency theory and applies to when people obey someone in authority because they give that person the power to make decisions for them ✓ and they are acting as an agent for the authority figure. ✓ An example is when soldiers act under orders rather than because of their own decision-making, or when Milgram's participants obeyed an order which they thought meant they were giving another person electric shocks. ✓ In-group behaviour refers to when people who are part of a group act according to group norms and rules that have been drawn up by the group members. ✓ They might wear a uniform or similar clothing or something that identifies them as part of a group. ✓ An example of in-group behaviour is when supporters of one football team wear the colours of the team and sing chants that they have developed. ✓

e Full marks are given here because the basic definition is there in each case, with some elaboration for the second mark. There are clear examples as well, with two examples for the explanation of 'agentic state'.

■ ■ ■

# Methodology

**(1) Give *one* strength and *one* weakness of surveys as a research method.**    (4 marks, AO3)

e There are 2 marks for the strength and 2 marks for the weakness. Do not just give a brief answer for each — be sure to expand your answer enough for the full 2 marks. For example, say what the strength is, and then say something else to explain it further or give an example.

## Answer

One strength is that a lot of people can be reached relatively cheaply by posting surveys or by handing them out in busy areas. Compared with an experiment, many participants can be reached and potentially can contribute data. ✓✓ A weakness is that there can be a poor response rate. When a lot of people are asked, it is likely that many will not post the questionnaire back, or that people will refuse to complete it if asked personally. ✓✓

🖉 A strength and a weakness are correctly identified, for 1 mark each, and there is some expansion in each case, so full marks.

**(2) An interview using a set list of questions was carried out with 20 people who happened to be in a town on a Tuesday afternoon. The aim was to find out whether people preferred those who were like them or were happier meeting and finding out about people who were different.**

**(a) What type of interview was being used?** (1 mark, AO3)

🖉 You have studied three types of interview and you need to choose the one that fits this stimulus material.

## Answer

Structured interview. ✓

🖉 This is the right answer — there is a set list of questions.

**(b) What sampling was used? Explain your answer.** (2 marks, AO3)

🖉 You have studied four sampling types, and two of these will fit the stimulus material, so choose one and briefly explain this choice for the second mark.

## Answer 1

This is volunteer sampling. ✓ Only those who stopped and agreed would have completed the interview, and this would mean the participants had volunteered and were self-selecting. ✓

🖉 This is right and the justification is clear, so both marks are given.

## Answer 2

Opportunity sampling. ✓

🖉 This is a right answer but it needs explaining — that only those in that town on a Tuesday afternoon are going to be in the sample. There could be 1 mark for saying 'opportunity', but it is also possible that this mark will only be given if it is clear that this knowledge is accompanied by understanding (you need to show you know what opportunity sampling is). Try to do more than just name the sampling method. For this answer, 1 mark is given.

**(c) Give two possible problems with the sampling method used.** (2 marks, AO3)

🖉 There is 1 mark for each problem, and 'give' does not mean you have to say anything about the problems. However, the problems need to be clear enough to be understood. The problems can be general issues concerning the sampling method, as the question does not say you have to relate to the stimulus material.

## Answer

Volunteer sampling means only those willing to take part do so; in this case, those with time will be in the sample, which means there is bias. ✓ Another related problem is that volunteers might be those of a certain gender, perhaps the same gender as the person carrying out the interviews, which again might mean bias. ✓

*e* There are 2 marks here, 1 for the factor of 'having time' and the other for 'gender'. The possible problems are clearly given.

**(d) Explain two advantages of using the type of interview used.** (4 marks, AO3)

*e* There are 2 marks for each advantage and nothing for disadvantages. To 'explain' the advantage you need to be clear about why it is good and how it relates to the type of interview, which in this case is structured interviewing.

## Answer

One advantage is the ease of analysis, because structured interviews ask all participants the same questions and the answers, therefore, can be confidently compared. ✓ Another advantage is that anyone can carry out the interview, because the questions are clearly listed and there is no deviation from them, ✓ so interviewers do not have to be trained in how to explore issues. ✓

*e* Only 3 marks are gained as there is not enough elaboration on the first advantage. The second advantage explains that, because there is no deviation from the questions, anyone can carry out the interviews, and then there is elaboration saying that this reduces the need for using only trained interviewers. The explanation of the first advantage, however, while noting that having the same questions means answers can be compared, does not elaborate on how this can be done or why this is useful. An elaboration could be that there is no problem with trying to compare the answers, unlike unstructured interviews, in which questions are explored further and differently for each respondent.

**(e) Explain one factor that might make the findings lack validity.** (2 marks, AO3)

*e* The question asks about validity, which refers to how 'real-life' the results will be. Consider one feature of the structured interview that would mean the results might be artificial, and make sure you say why this would be the case, so that you get the 2 marks. The question does not ask you to consider that particular structured interview (such as the sampling or the situation), but you could do.

## Answer

The interview might lack validity because the interviewer will take the respondent through the set questions even if there is more that the respondent wants to say about the issues. ✓ This restricts the respondent's answers and means that they are limited, so it is likely that they lack validity. The answers will in some ways be forced because of the questions. ✓ In some structured interviews some questions are closed questions, which would mean even more forced-choice answers.

🖉 This answer is thorough and gets both marks. The factor is identified as the restrictions that set questions impose, and the answer then explains this more fully by saying that this means the answer cannot be expanded beyond the question, which in turn means that 'real' answers might not be given. You can see that even though there are only 2 marks, the answer has to be reasonably thorough to make sure the points are clear.

**(f) Given what you know about social identity, what would you expect to find from the interview? Explain your answer.** (2 marks, AO3)

🖉 You do not have to explain social identity theory here, but you could summarise it briefly and then link to the aim of the interview and what results would be expected.

## Answer 1

You would expect that people prefer their own in-group. ✓

🖉 This is limited but is a brief statement of what would be expected and is accurate, so is likely to get 1 mark.

## Answer 2

Social identity theory suggests that self-esteem comes from being in a group with others and identifying with that group — which is then treated as better than an out-group so that self-esteem is good. So it would be expected that people prefer people from their in-group, operationalised as being 'like them', rather than people from the out-group, operationalised as people who are 'different'. ✓ ✓

🖉 This answer gets both marks because the link to social identity theory is clear and the question is answered clearly too — people are more likely to like people in their in-group than those in their out-group.

■ ■ ■

# Content

**(1) What is meant by the term 'obedience'?** (2 marks, AO1)

🖉 You need to give a definition of obedience. A simple definition will gain 1 mark and a more detailed definition will gain the 2 marks.

## Answer

Obedience is when people obey others in authority. ✓

🔎 This gets 1 mark because it is right but not worth both marks. It is not enough to say that obedience is when people obey, but saying that they obey others in authority is enough for 1 mark. For full marks, this needs more detail, such as mentioning that obeying means you are in an agentic state, or saying that it differs from conformity in that someone is acting upon orders and might not agree. More needs to be said, such as 'following orders' rather than 'obey', because 'obey' is obvious. It is good to give an example, such as when someone moves a car because a parking attendant tells them to.

**(2) Describe Milgram's agency theory of obedience.** (4 marks, AO1)

🔎 There are 4 marks here, all for describing what is meant by the agency theory. An example is a good idea, but keep it short as it is worth no more than 1 mark. However, it helps to illustrate your answer and show that you understand the theory.

## Answer

In Milgram's study, the participants denied to themselves that they were responsible for their actions. They allowed the experimenter to take responsibility for what was happening. When you are not acting under your own control but because of the orders of someone else, you are their agent, and this is called being in an agentic state. ✓✓

🔎 2 marks are awarded here for saying what an agentic state is, although the answer is not well focused on the question. The other 2 marks could be gained by linking this to Milgram's study and showing that the participants said they felt they had to continue and were just obeying orders. This was his agency theory of obedience — that people were not making their own decisions. The answer could have said that the opposite of the agentic state is being autonomous and acting on one's own decisions, whereas being in an agentic state means doing what someone in authority says, which is probably necessary in order for society to function. This could possibly be due to someone being brought up in that way, or possibly because of inherited tendencies.

**(3) Evaluate social identity theory as an explanation of prejudice.** (4 marks, AO2)

🔎 Note that for 'evaluate' questions you do not have to describe at all. Assume that the examiner knows what the theory is. All 4 marks are for evaluation. You could say that another theory explains prejudice better or contradicts this one, or you could criticise the research methods used to arrive at the theory (perhaps researchers used laboratory experiments that are not valid). If you mention an alternative theory there is likely to be only 1 mark, because if you then start looking more at that alternative theory you are addressing a different question.

## Answer

Many studies have shown that we prefer our in-group and are less interested in any out-group, and their findings are evidence for the theory. Tajfel did a lot of work in this area, and others have too. It seems that we boost our self-esteem by siding with an in-group, which means going against an out-group. So social identity theory (SIT) seems a reasonable explanation and we have evidence for it. ✓ It can also explain the findings of other studies of prejudice, even if they are said to be about another theory. For example, Minard carried out a study of miners. The study could be explained by saying that the miners were an in-group when working, but when above ground, they were no longer an in-group (not being 'miners' any more but going home to different roles). ✓ Also Sherif's study at Robbers Cave, although arriving at the theory of realistic conflict as an explanation of prejudice, did look at in-group and out-group behaviour between the Rattlers and Eagles and found out-group hostility, as social identity theory predicts. ✓ However, much of the research was done using experiments and falsely formed groups, so the conclusions might not be valid. ✓

*e* Full marks are gained here. 1 mark is awarded for saying that there is a lot of evidence (although this needs elaboration, as is done here, by giving Tajfel). A further mark is given for the Minard example and showing how SIT can explain it. Minard is probably a new study for you and shows that it is useful to go beyond your textbook. But you could add more about evidence (e.g. experiments are reliable) to get the final mark. Another mark is for the reference to the theory being useful in explaining Sherif's findings. The final mark is for the methodological criticism of the lack of validity.

■ ■ ■

# Studies in detail

**(1) Describe Hofling et al. (1966) — a study from the social approach.**       (5 marks, AO1)

*e* Note that just describing what was done in the study (the procedure), or what was found (the results or findings), is not enough for all 5 marks. One way of getting the marks is to assume that up to 2 marks can be gained for saying why the study was done, which is the aim. Up to 2 more marks can be gained by saying what was done, which is the procedure. There are up to 2 marks for saying what was found (the results). A maximum of 2 marks can also be earned for giving the conclusions. There are more ways than one to get the 5 marks. These ideas apply if the question asks for the whole study to be described. There could, however, be a question about one of the elements (e.g. procedure, results) that asks for more than 2 marks, so you need to prepare more, as is advised in the content section of this book.

## Answer

Hofling studied a group of 22 nurses in the main field experiment. The nurses were on duty and were given instructions over the phone by a doctor who wanted them to give a patient a dosage of a drug — however, this dosage would have been too high. ✓ Although the nurses should not have taken instructions over the phone, and they should have checked the dosage, 21 out of the 22 nurses obeyed the doctor. ✓ They were stopped before the drug was administered, and there was no real medication in any case. ✓ The study was to find out whether nurses would obey orders when they knew they should not. ✓

The first mark is for the procedure, although a little more detail would have earned 2 marks. The main result (21 out of 22 obeyed) is given, and gets 1 mark. A mark is awarded for the information that they were stopped and in any case there was no real drug, as this is elaboration upon the procedure. A further mark could have been gained by drawing a clear conclusion about obedience to authority. The aim is given at the end and gets a mark too. So 4 marks are awarded out of 5. More could have been said about the findings, and 'findings' means results and/or conclusions. Note with 2 procedure marks having been given, there are no more available given the likelihood of there being a maximum of 2 marks for this element of the study.

**(2) Evaluate Hofling et al. (1966) — a study from the social approach.** (5 marks, AO2)

Evaluation of studies can come in many forms. You can give ethical issues (good and/or bad), alternative theories or studies, methodological problems (such as the reliability of experiments or the limitations of case studies) or criticisms of the study itself. Be sure to write enough for 5 marks. You are trying to say five things, although it is possible to gain more than 1 mark for a good, well made point. This question could be AO3, because the methodology and study findings are going to be evaluated, but if the answer includes evaluation using another study or a theory, such as saying that the study reinforces Milgram's agency theory, it could be argued that that is AO2.

## Answer

The nurses were carrying out instructions in response to the doctor's authority. As part of the study, nurses in a control group were asked if they would obey instructions such as those given in the study, and they all said they would not. This shows that the situation we are in and the social pressure at the time influences our behaviour, which is a useful contribution. ✓ As this study was a field study and took place in a real hospital with real nurses, it was thought to be stronger evidence of obedience than Milgram's artificial laboratory study. The study has ecological validity (validity with regard to setting and situation). ✓✓ Nurses were taken from different hospitals, so possibly generalisation is okay, but all the nurses were female, so there may have been an issue in generalising to male nurses. The obedience could have been because the 'doctor' was male and the nurse female. ✓✓

1 mark is achieved for pointing out the usefulness of the contribution, and 2 marks for comparing the study with Milgram's and showing that Hofling's study is arguably more valid. This is a double mark because there is quite a bit of information, and if you gave just some of it you would get 1 mark. A further double mark is given because the issue of generalisation is given in some detail, with examples as to why it might be a problem. So this answer gets all 5 marks.

**(3) Describe the findings (results and/or conclusions) of either Reicher and Haslam (2003/2006), the Sherif et al. (1954) Robbers Cave study or Tajfel et al. (1970/1971) — studies from the social approach.** (5 marks, AO1)

The results and/or conclusions (findings) of one of the listed studies are asked for. 5 marks are quite a lot, so details are needed. It would be wise to give both the results and the conclusions. Focus on results and/or conclusions and do not describe what happened in the study. Do make sure it is identifiable, but it should be if the results and/or conclusions are accurate. In this book Reicher and Haslam (2003//2006) has been explained but the other studies are included here for your interest or in case you covered one of them in your course instead of Reicher and Haslam.

## Answer for Reicher and Haslam (2006)

Reicher and Haslam found that participants who were given the role of prisoner formed an in-group and worked as a group as well as identifying with the group. ✓ However, the guards did not form into a group and did not work as a team. ✓ There were five guards, and it was noticed that the strongest personalities were among the prisoners, which may have led to the strength of the prisoners. ✓ As the prisoners grew stronger as a group, they overcame the authority of the guards and a commune-style system was developed by agreement of all the participants. ✓ However, this did not last, and by the end of the study the participants had agreed that they needed a strong system to achieve the aims they had been set. ✓

🖉 This answer works through the results and is clear and detailed. No real conclusions are given, except perhaps the fact that the strongest personalities being found among the prisoners might have led to the results — though that in itself is like a result. Each point gets a mark, as it is clearly expressed. More about the conclusions would have added marks if they were needed. For example, they found that social identity theory was supported by the findings of the study and identification with an in-group helped with decision-making and forming group norms.

## Answer for Sherif et al. (1954) the Robbers Cave study

Sherif et al. found that the boys formed two in-groups and quickly formed leader–follower relations as well as setting up group norms so that decisions could be made. ✓ Once each in-group knew about the other, they were quickly hostile towards the out-group and started to call them names, for example. ✓ They wanted to compete with the out-group. Competition led to hostility and friction. ✓ Finally, working towards superordinate goals reduced the friction, but only after they had to work together for quite a few such goals. ✓✓

🖉 This answer also gets the full 5 marks because of the detail given. The last point about superordinate goals gets a double mark because it mentions that more than one super-ordinate goal had to be worked towards for reduction of prejudice, which is an elaboration of the point about working towards superordinate goals. Also, the use of the term enriches that part of the answer.

## Answer for Tajfel et al. (1970)

Tajfel et al. set up minimal groups by falsely suggesting that individuals liked either Klee or Kandinsky and that that put them into a special group. He set up a study where the participants had to give rewards either to their own group members or to individuals from the other group, the out-group. It was found that even when minimal groups were formed, the members of the in-group still favoured their own members against out-group members. ✓

🔁 This only gets 1 mark because a lot more detail is needed about the results and/or conclusions. The answer is spoiled because a lot of it focuses on the procedure of the study, which is not asked for, so that bit gets no marks. This shows the importance of answering the question.

■ ■ ■

# Key issue

**(1) Read the source below. Then explain what is being said, using concepts from the social approach.** (6 marks, AO2)

> Fighting broke out between two local villages when a visiting rugby team from one of the villages won an annual competition by 28 points. At first, the fight was only between two of the players who had clashed during the match, but soon the fighting spread and police had to be called. Elders from one of the villages explained that there had been prejudice between the two villages for years, ever since a factory was built near one village. This had brought good road links and jobs, whereas the other village was in another valley and did not have the same advantages.

🔁 This extract is clearly focusing on groups, which suggests that social identity theory is a good one to choose in order to explain the extract. If you have studied the Sherif study, you could also look at the idea that competition leads to hostility between groups and working towards superordinate goals can help to reduce the hostility. If you have studied Tajfel's study about minimal groups, you can use the findings to help to explain the extract. The Reicher and Haslam study also looks at the success of an in-group structure, so can be used. When studying the social approach you will have looked at what the approach is about in general, such as how behaviour has to be understood in terms of groups and cultures, and those concepts can also be useful for this answer. Remember to refer to the source at least once in your answer to show you are clearly focusing on the question.

## Answer

Social identity theory claims that prejudice arises when an in-group becomes hostile to an out-group, possibly to enhance the self-esteem of the in-group. ✓ In the source passage, the villagers in each case would probably form an in-group, including not only those who were team members but the whole village. ✓ This would be more likely if one village were seen to be better off than the other, as was the case here. This is an example of scapegoating — where people are blamed for problems they are not responsible for, and prejudice forms. ✓ Prejudice can lead to aggression through frustration, and economic disadvantages can lead to frustration. ✓

*ⓔ* Two concepts of how prejudice might occur (SIT and scapegoating) are given here, and each earns marks. In each case, 1 mark is for giving the concept accurately, and for SIT, 1 mark is for linking well to the passage. A fourth mark is given for suggesting that frustration might cause the aggression. This links to the frustration–aggression hypothesis, which you may not have studied, but is a good, relevant point from social psychology and shows that you can bring in material from anywhere within the approach. Further marks could have been scored by adding that in this case, the villages were in competition, but if another situation arose where they had to work together (to solve a superordinate goal, for example), prejudice might be reduced, which links to Sherif's study. Ideas from crowd behaviour could also have been used successfully here, as well as evidence from the other studies that are suggested for the 'Studies in detail' section of the course. If you stick to what you have learned in the course, that is fine — and you could have gone into more depth about social categorisation, social comparison and social identity, using the theory to get more marks.

**(2) Social psychology can be used to help us understand key issues in psychology. Describe *one* such key issue.** (4 marks, AO1)

*ⓔ* The main point here is to describe the issue, not the psychology that helps to explain it. Avoid mentioning studies, theories or concepts as far as you can, because they are the explanations of the issue, not the description. Sometimes you have to use concepts, because the issue is about such concepts — for example, if you choose prejudice. However, most concepts can be avoided — for example, refer to two groups in conflict, not to in-group and out-group, if you are talking about football hooliganism.

## Answer

In recent years there have been occasions when members of armed forces have been charged as individuals for brutal acts. ✓ One example is when US soldiers were photographed treating prisoners in the Abu Ghraib prison in Iraq in a humiliating and brutal way. ✓ Soldiers are supposed to treat prisoners of war carefully and with respect for their position, and there are rules and conventions. ✓ The pictures were published in the media and there was a general outcry from around the world against soldiers using their position of power in such a way. It was hard to understand how they could do this, given their training. ✓

*ⓔ* This answer is clear enough and marks are given quite quickly, as it is not easy to stick to describing only the issue — which is how this could happen and what would make them do it. The first mark is for the general idea that soldiers should not commit brutal acts, though this is not yet fully explained in the answer. The second mark is for the actual example. The third mark is for one side of the issue — that soldiers are not supposed to do this. The fourth mark is for the actual issue — that it is hard to understand why this would happen, with the implication that such behaviour needs to be explained.

**(3) Use concepts and ideas from the social approach to explain one key issue that you have studied. In your answer make the key issue clear.** (6 marks, AO1)

📝 This question is asking you to choose a key issue and apply what you know about social psychology to help to explain the issue. The marks are AO1 marks because you will be describing what you have learned rather than applying it to a novel situation, as is done in question 1 in this section. Use terminology as much as you can, to give a good answer. You can use studies to help to explain the concepts. Here answers are given on two issues other than the Abu Ghraib situation that was chosen as the key issue for this book. This is because it is useful for you to know about other issues, in order to prepare for an issue you might be presented with in the examination. You do not have to know these other issues or explanations, but it is useful to know a little bit more about the approach for this section.

## Answer on football hooliganism

A key issue that can be explained using ideas from the social approach is football hooliganism. One concept is deindividuation. People do things when they are anonymous that they would not otherwise do. ✓ They get carried away by the behaviour of the crowd around them, and follow the actions of another person. This idea of being carried away has been called social contagion. ✓ Ethnocentricity is another concept. This is the rejection of the out-group and the focus on the in-group. ✓ In a football crowd, the in-group would be the supporters of the team the individual supports, and the out-group would be supporters of the other team. ✓ So whatever the in-group is doing, that person would follow, and this would lead to prejudice towards the out-group — and possibly violence. ✓ Social identity theory explains that people identify with their in-group and think positively about its members, whereas they think negatively about the out-group members. This helps to increase their self-esteem. ✓ Football supporters are out-groups if they support the 'other' team, so there would be hostility towards the out-group.

📝 This answer gets all the marks. The first mark is for the idea of deindividuation, which is summarised to show it is understood. The second mark is for social contagion, another theory of crowd behaviour. You may not have come across these two concepts, because you have not prepared this key issue — and in fact you can discuss football hooliganism without mentioning these concepts. Just use the concepts you know and have prepared. A third mark is given for the link to in-groups and out-groups, and another mark for the elaboration of this point by showing how the idea of in-group and out-group fits with football supporters. The fifth mark is good because there is a link to violence, which is what hooliganism is about. And the final mark is for elaborating on the idea of social identity theory and mentioning the link with self-esteem.

## Answer on crowd behaviour

Control of crowd behaviour is something that has been investigated in the social approach. In particular, in this country (and others) football crowds have become violent, and this has spoilt enjoyment for many and cost a lot in terms of policing (and injuries). The social approach has shown that people are deindividuated in a crowd and may do things they would not otherwise do. ✓ If video cameras are used, or if only season ticket-holders are allowed into the game, this might prevent deindividuation, because individuals could be identified. ✓ This should help to prevent football hooliganism. Crowds can also be affected by emotional contagion, where emotions spread to those around, and previously calm individuals may become violent. ✓ A way of avoiding this is to keep the crowd calm. If people do not all stand together but stadiums are all-seating with no standing, this might help to avoid pressure. It could be that reactions come from biological stresses, which means social psychology is not the only explanation. ✓ Social psychology studies can be experimental, which means the situation can be unnatural and so not applicable to real life. However, many studies are done in the field as observations, and much can be discovered from these because they are studying real crowd situations and real crowd behaviour, so there is validity. ✓

🖉 This is a good answer up to a point, and at the end it starts to consider evaluation. There are some good points, such as biological factors being important, and also the fact that many studies are not done in natural situations so there is no validity, which means findings are in doubt and 2 marks are given for this evaluation. Deindividuation gets a mark, and another mark is given for elaboration, as the answer suggests how to avoid the problem. A mark is given for social contagion too, so 5 marks are given in all. Other marks could be achieved by talking about realistic conflict if the crowd has formed because of some pressure or problem. The idea of superordinate goals could be discussed in that case, helping to show how to reduce pressure. Football crowds are mentioned, so the idea of in-group and out-group could be used, as in the previous answer.

■ ■ ■

# Practical

For the social approach you will have carried out either a questionnaire or an interview. Answer the following questions with your practical in mind.

**(1) (a) What is the aim of the practical?** (2 marks, AO3)

🖉 Expect to give the aim of each of your practicals — the aim usually has 2 marks. Just be clear, giving the research method if appropriate and what you were trying to find out — this often includes a brief mention of the IV and the DV, but this might not be appropriate. You do not need to give full detail of these variables.

## Answer

My questionnaire was to find out, using both open and closed questions, if people think those in their in-group are better than others who are in the out-group. This is to test the social identity theory. ✓✓

This is fine, as it gives the research method, the types of questions and the independent variable as well as the overall aim of testing the theory. Well worth the 2 marks.

**(b) Give two examples of what was asked/what was in the interview schedule.** (2 marks, AO3)

 You need to give two questions here — either questionnaire or interview questions. Here it is assumed that the practical was a questionnaire to look at social identity theory. You don't need to be exact about what you actually asked, just make sure the questions are appropriate to your aim.

## Answer

Do you like people in your group better than those in other groups?  Yes    No ✓

When you are with people you don't know very well, does that make you feel less confident?  Yes    No ✓

 These two questions are fine and would work. You might think of problems with them, but the idea is just to test the sort of questions that could be asked and they don't have to be perfect.

**(c) Why did you include personal data?** (2 marks, AO3)

 Personal data are data about the individual rather than about the IV. The question asks you to talk about why that is needed, rather than which personal data you asked for. You could answer by referring to the actual personal data you gathered — but remember to say why.

## Answer

Personal data are needed to check the data against. For example, I asked about gender because I wanted to know if there is a gender difference in in-group preferences. ✓

 This gets 1 mark because the example makes the first sentence clear, but on its own the first sentence is not particularly helpful. The answer needed to say what 'check against' means. Another example might have got you another mark, if the example was detailed enough. Or the answer could say more about what personal data are.

**(d) Explain one ethical decision you made.** (2 marks, AO3)

 Choose one ethical issue you considered — even if you did not address it well. Then explain the issue and what you did about it (or why you did not).

## Answer

I was careful to get informed consent. I put standardised instructions on the top of my questionnaire and said it was about in-group and out-group behaviour and that the findings would only be used for my course. I said that no names were required and that data were confidential. This told the respondent about the study, so they were informed. Then I just asked them if it was okay to continue, which meant consent was given and informed. ✓ ✓

🖉 This is a thorough answer and gets the 2 marks.

**(e) Choose whether a survey is a reliable or a valid research method and explain your answer.** (2 marks, AO3)

🖉 Choose to look at either validity or reliability and then, having chosen, discuss your research method with that issue in mind.

## Answer

A survey has good reliability because there are set questions and they are repeated for all respondents. So the answers, which often give quantitative data, can be compared. ✓ Questions should be clear, following a pilot study, so that if they were asked again the same responses would be found. ✓

🖉 There is enough here for the 2 marks. This answer clearly shows understanding of what reliability is and mentions the issues of closed questions, comparability and a pilot study, all of which are useful issues with regard to reliability.

# The cognitive approach

## Definitions

**(1) Outline one factor that a definition of the cognitive approach might include.** (3 marks, AO1)

> This question asks for an outline, which is a brief description. One way of getting 1 mark is to give an example, but you would need to outline the factor first. Think of something about the approach and write it down. Then explain it a bit more to elaborate. Then think of an example of this factor within the approach.

### Answer

The mind/brain processes information. ✓ We take information in, and then it is subjected to mental processes. There is input, processing and then output. ✓ For example, we take information in via the senses, process it according to the multi-store model of memory, through two stores — the short-term store and the long-term store — and then there is an output if we remember the information. ✓

> This is a clear and concise answer. 1 mark is given for the factor, in this case that we process information. 1 mark is awarded for linking this to the processing of information and for expanding on this by mentioning input, processing and output. There could have been 2 marks here if the idea of mental processes had been expanded as well. The example of the multi-store model gained the final mark as it is clear and used effectively. Note that just saying that the multi-store model is an example is not enough — you have to show how it is an example.

**(2) Tick two of the following statements that are features of the cognitive approach.** (2 marks, AO1)
**(a) According to the cognitive approach we are guided strongly by our unconscious** ☐
**(b) The approach holds that there are similarities in the ways computers and brains operate** ☐
**(c) The approach holds that information is processed by the brain; there is input, processing and output** ☐
**(d) The approach focuses on why we behave as we do in groups** ☐

> This is straightforward in that there are two correct statements and two are not about the cognitive approach. This would be a multiple-choice question and you would put ticks in the boxes provided.

### Answer

**(a) According to the cognitive approach we are guided strongly by our unconscious** ☐

(b) **The approach holds that there are similarities in the ways computers and brains operate** ☑ ✓

(c) **The approach holds that information is processed by the brain; there is input, processing and output** ☑ ✓

(d) **The approach focuses on why we behave as we do in groups** ☐

*e* These choices are correct, for 2 marks.

(3) **Using information from cognitive psychology, explain what is meant by saying that the information processing approach could include input, processing and output.** (3 marks, AO1)

*e* You would expect to be asked about the cognitive approach in general, but prepare for questions like this to help with detail. You can use one of the memory theories you studied or one of the forgetting theories — or any other ideas and concepts you know about.

## Answer 1

The levels of processing approach suggests that what is input, such as the type of question, leads to different processing ✓ and different output, such as whether the 'yes' or 'no' response is activated and how this affects whether a word is recognised or not. ✓ For example, if a question asks whether one word rhymes with another word, the words are input ✓ and the processing involves whether the words rhyme or not. ✓ This is likely to include referring to previously stored information in some way. Following the processing a 'yes' or 'no' response occurs, which is the output. ✓

*e* This answer is given five ticks, although there is some repetition in the answer. The ticks are given to show where marks are possible.

## Answer 2

The interference theory of forgetting shows how information is input, processing occurs and then this processing affects the output. The multi-store model suggests that there is short-term and long-term memory and that interference in long-term memory depends on what has been stored previously. ✓ Information is input through the senses — sight, sound, taste and so on ✓ — and then processing takes place. Processing is through the short-term and then, for storage to take place more permanently, the long-term memory (LTM). ✓ Then there is output, depending on what is to be recalled, but output can be affected by interference at the processing stage. ✓ This means there is forgetting.

*e* This answer also gets full marks and there is an additional mark just to show where marks might be given. The theory is clearly linked to input, processing and output.

■ ■ ■

# Methodology

**(1) Outline _one_ strength and _one_ weakness of the experiment as a research method.**
(4 marks, AO3)

> *e* There are 2 marks for the strength and 2 marks for the weakness. Don't just give a brief answer for each: be sure to expand it enough for the full 2 marks. For example, say what the strength is and then expand on what you mean.

## Answer

A strength is that it is well controlled. A weakness is that you cannot see natural behaviour, as the experiment is in a laboratory. ✓

> *e* The weakness gets 1 mark because the answer clearly and effectively communicates that natural behaviour is not found in a laboratory. For the additional mark, this needs elaborating, perhaps mentioning the lack of validity, or saying that the unnatural situation means that what is being measured is not 'normal'. The strength does not earn a mark. The answer needs to say *what* is well controlled, and how that means that a study can be repeated to see if the same results are found, which means it has reliability, or at least something about why good controls are a strength.

**(2) Name three types of experiment.**
(1 mark, AO3)

> *e* There might be more marks for a question like this, but it is more likely that there would be just 1 mark as the question only asks for a list.

## Answer

Field, laboratory and natural. ✓

> *e* This is fine, and the question does not need any more, but it is always a good idea to spell everything out and add 'experiment' to make the answer complete.

**(3) Here are some data from a study.**

*Number of words recognised from a list of 30, according to whether the words were processed structurally, phonemically or semantically (repeated measures design)*

| Participant | Structurally processed (Is the word in capitals?) | Phonemically processed (Does the word rhyme with...?) | Semantically processed (Does the word fit in this sentence?) |
|---|---|---|---|
| 1 | 3 | 7 | 21 |
| 2 | 4 | 9 | 18 |
| 3 | 2 | 10 | 24 |
| 4 | 8 | 12 | 16 |

| Participant | Structurally processed (Is the word in capitals?) | Phonemically processed (Does the word rhyme with...?) | Semantically processed (Does the word fit in this sentence?) |
|---|---|---|---|
| 5 | 5 | 14 | 20 |
| 6 | 7 | 8 | 17 |
| 7 | 10 | 12 | 16 |
| 8 | 4 | 16 | 18 |
| 9 | 3 | 8 | 12 |
| 10 | 4 | 8 | 24 |
| Mean | 5 | 10.4 | 18.6 |
| Median | 4 | 9.5 | 18 |
| Mode | 4 | 8 | 16/18/24 |
| Range | 8 | 9 | 12 |

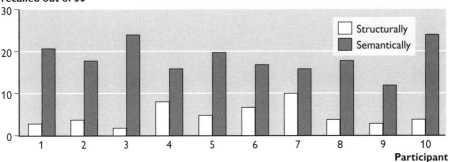

*Number of words recalled, whether processed structurally or semantically*

**(3) (a) Which type of processing led to more words being recalled on average? Explain your answer.** (2 marks, AO3)

You need to choose one or more of the averages (mean, median or mode, though when the word 'average' is used it usually refers to the mean, so that would be a suitable choice) and give the figures to explain your answer.

## Answer

The mean average shows that the semantic processing gave the most recall, the phonemic the next best recall and structural processing the worst recall. ✓ The worst recall gave a mean average of 5.0 words of the 30 (structural), the next best gave a mean average of 10.4 (phonemic) and the best recall gave a mean average of 18.6 words out of 30. ✓ The median and the mode showed the same pattern. ✓

🖉 This answer is thorough and gives the answer in figures as well as words, which strengthens it. Where possible, include figures in such an answer. There are three ticks, though only 2 marks are available.

**(b) Summarise what the graph shows.**                    (2 marks, AO3)

🖉 You need to show the trends the graph illustrates. Say enough for the 2 marks, so more than just one brief sentence.

## Answer

The graph shows that every participant recalls more words when asked if a word fits into a sentence (semantic processing) than if asked whether a word is in capital letters (structural processing). ✓ In all but one case twice as many (or more) words are recalled when using semantic processing, which shows the size of the difference. ✓

🖉 The first sentence is the main answer, but you need more for the second mark — looking at the size of the difference is a good idea as it is a clear feature of this graph.

**(c) Explain how to find the median and the mode of a set of numbers.**   (4 marks, AO3)

🖉 If you needed to, you could work out how the two measures of central tendency are calculated, because the table shows this. There are 2 marks for each explanation, so you could use an example to illustrate for the second mark.

## Answer

The median is the middle score of a set of scores, ✓ and if there is an even number of scores (such as 10, as here), the median is in the middle of the scores and has to be calculated (such as midway between scores 5 and 6 here). ✓ If there is an odd number of scores (such as 11), the median is in the middle and it is easier to find, as it will be the score at position 6. The mode is the score found most often, ✓ and to calculate it means looking to see which score appears the most times. ✓ If there is not just one score in this position, but more, all those scores appear against the mode — there is no single mode. This is the case for the semantic processing condition in this example.

🖉 There is more here than is needed for the 4 marks, because the first mark is given for a basic definition of the two terms and then another mark is given for elaboration. Don't assume that this quick early mark is being awarded, and give more explanation, as is done here. It is always better to show understanding of the issue(s) in as much depth as possible bearing in mind time restraints, of course.

■ ■ ■

# Content

**(1) Outline *one* theory of forgetting.**                    (3 marks, AO1)

🄴 Giving one theory of forgetting earns you the first mark. Then there are 2 more marks for expanding on your answer. Say what the theory is, and make sure you say enough about it for the 2 extra marks.

## Answer

Retrieval failure — the cues for recall ✓ do not match the encoding that takes place in memory. ✓

🄴 Retrieval failure due to lack of cues scores 1 mark for the theory, and the additional information about cues not matching encoding gets another 1 mark. However, this is not a clear outline of a theory of forgetting. You would need to be clearer, to talk about cue-dependent forgetting, and to mention state and context dependency. This answer scores 2 marks out of 3, but only just.

**(2) Evaluate *one* theory or model of memory in terms of *two* of the following criteria: methodological issues, ethical issues, alternative theories, research evidence for contradictory claims or its practical application.** (6 marks, AO2)

🄴 You have to do two things here and there are 6 marks, so there are 3 marks for each task. Choose one of the criteria (e.g. ethical issues) and say three things about ethical issues in relation to your chosen theory of memory. Then choose one of the other criteria (e.g. alternative theories) and say three things about alternative theories. You can get marks by elaborating a point, so, for example, if you choose ethics and talk about one ethical issue in depth, you could gain more than 1 mark, or you could gain marks by looking at different ethical issues.

## Answer

The multi-store model has stimulated much research into the mind to identify exactly how memory is used and stored. This stimulated research by Baddeley and Hitch, who came up with the working memory (WM) model. ✓ The WM model expands short-term memory (STM) to look at four different areas. ✓ These include an articulatory loop, a visuospatial scratchpad and a central executive. ✓ Research is based on experimental evidence, which is said to lack validity as artificial tasks are used. ✓

🄴 The first criterion covered is alternative theory, and for this all 3 marks are gained. 1 mark is for the mention of the model having stimulated research such as the working memory model. The second mark is for mentioning the four areas of the working model, and the third mark for elaborating on this. The second criterion is methodological issues, and a mark is given for mentioning the artificial nature of experiments used. This could have been expanded by means of an example, or at least explained more fully, for the final 2 marks. For example, it could be said that learning lists underwater, as was done in Godden and Baddeley's study, is not a normal thing to do.

**section**

**(3) For _one_ model/theory of memory that you have studied, complete the following table.**                         (3 marks, AO1)

| Instruction regarding the model or theory | Answer |
|---|---|
| Identify the model/theory | |
| State one aspect of the model/theory | |
| State one problem with the model/theory | |

There is 1 mark for each element. You do not need to say much for 1 mark. The first mark is for naming the model (or identifying it if you cannot recall the name of the theory or the name(s) of the researchers). The second mark is for saying something about that model — for example, if looking at the multi-store model, saying that the focus is on two stores: STM and LTM. The third mark is for saying something to criticise it.

## Answer

| Instruction regarding the model or theory | Answer |
|---|---|
| Identify the model/theory | Levels of processing, Craik and Lockhart (1972) |
| State one aspect of the model/theory | Three levels of processing are found — structural, phonemic and semantic |
| State one problem with the model/theory | Circular, in not really explaining anything; better recall comes from deeper processing, and we show deeper processing by pointing to better recall |

Each of the above answers scores 1 mark. When only 1 mark is available, remember that you do not have to write a great deal. This answer gets full marks.

**(4) Compare the two models/theories of forgetting that you have studied for your course.**                         (4 marks, AO2)

You need to make four comparison points, clearly stating both sides of the point, to get the full marks. You could consider research methods (similarities or differences), what is being looked at (similarities or differences), the historical time when the theory/model was developed (similar or different), or any other feature you think of. Of course, both will be within cognitive psychology but that is fairly obvious, as is the fact that both are about forgetting, so avoid such answers.

## Answer

Cue-dependent forgetting is similar to interference theory because both are studied using lists of words to see under what circumstances words are forgotten. Godden and Baddeley (1975) asked divers to learn lists of words either on land or underwater and then to recall them. To test retroactive and proactive interference, different word lists are given and recalled (either the first or the second list is recalled), which is a similar procedure. ✓✓ Both theories use experiments to study the explanation of forgetting, and often the experiments are laboratory experiments. ✓ Cue-dependent theory considers features in the environment and how they affect remembering and forgetting, whereas interference theory looks at features in the brain to see how forgetting is affected. ✓ However, cue-dependent theory does consider how the absence of the right cues for processing causes forgetting, so both are about information processing, as would be expected in cognitive psychology. ✓

🖉 This answer gets the 4 marks and there are possibly 5 marks, but some of the points are not clearly made so only just get the mark. Aim for a more complete point each time. For example, saying that they both use words does not quite get the mark, though giving the two clear elaboration points afterwards means 2 marks are given together then. Saying that both use laboratory experiments is also rather weak but just gets the mark here. Include something more, e.g. they both have a clearly operationalised IV and a measurable DV. The comment about both looking at information processing but one being more concerned with internal processes is a useful one and there is some elaboration. It could, however, have been clearer, because cues are recorded from the cognitive environment in cue-dependent forgetting, which is an internal feature.

■ ■ ■

# Studies in detail

**(1) You will have studied Godden and Baddeley's divers study and one other from Peterson and Peterson, Craik and Tulving and Ramponi et al. Compare Godden and Baddeley's study with one of the other three in terms of the methodology used.** (6 marks, AO3)

🖉 When asked to compare, you need to give similarities and/or differences, and for this question you need to look at methodology. A good idea is to think of all aspects of the methodology of one of the studies and say how the other is the same or different in that aspect. Another way is to think of methodological issues and say how the two are similar or different with regard to those issues. Remember to compare and to say explicitly that one is 'XXX' (some feature), whereas the other is 'YYY' (a different feature), for example. In this guide the studies chosen are Godden and Baddeley (1975) and Craik and Tulving (1975), but the other two from the course are given here in case you studied them instead. Also knowing a bit about them will be useful, as you might be able to use the study in the key issue or in evaluation. You do not have to know another study, though, other than Godden and Baddeley and one of the other three.

## Answer 1: Godden and Baddeley compared with Peterson and Peterson

Both of the studies look at cognitive processes, so in that way they are similar. However, Peterson and Peterson focus more on remembering, with Godden and Baddeley looking at forgetting. They both used experiments as the research method. ✓ Godden and Baddeley used a repeated measures design and Peterson and Peterson set up two experimental procedures in their study, one of which used independent groups, so the designs were different. ✓ Godden and Baddeley used lists of words and Peterson and Peterson had lists of consonants that they used one by one, so in a way the two were similar because they both used words or letters that were recalled or not. ✓ Both studies were very carefully controlled so that only the IV was varied, and the DV could be said to be caused by the variation in the IV. ✓ For example, Godden and Baddeley tried to ensure that moving from water to land for one group did not cause disruption that would not apply to the other group, ✓ and Peterson and Peterson were careful not to use the same consonants more than once for each participant. ✓

> 🖉 The first mark is given for saying they both use experiments, though it could have done with more detail. The detail comes later, however, when cause and effect and controls are mentioned. The second mark is for comparing the designs, and this time there is almost enough for 2 marks — 1 is given, though, because of that fairly quick first mark. The third mark is for saying their stimulus materials are similar and the fourth for mentioning good controls and elaborating a bit with comments about the IV and DV. The fifth and sixth marks are for giving the detail about the controls, one example for each study. Notice that the first two points about cognitive processes and focusing on memory or forgetting are good comparison points but get no marks, because this question was about methodology.

## Answer 2: Godden and Baddeley compared with Ramponi et al.

Both Godden and Baddeley and Ramponi et al. use experiments as their research methodology, and both are trying to isolate single variables that they can test to find out about cognitive processes. ✓ Godden and Baddeley use fewer participants than Ramponi et al., because there are not many divers they can use, whereas Ramponi et al. have a large sample of both older and younger participants. ✓ Godden and Baddeley use 18 participants and altogether Ramponi et al. use 96. ✓ Both studies involve memory testing of some sort using words somehow, so in that way they are similar. ✓ Godden and Baddeley work in the field with their participants in that they are diving in any case and the study works around them, whereas Ramponi et al. set the whole study up for the purposes of gathering the data exclusively — which makes the two studies different with regard to validity. ✓ It could be said that the Godden and Baddeley study was more valid because the divers were doing what they did anyway, but they did not usually learn lists of words with special equipment, so really it was no more valid than Ramponi et al. ✓

📝 Again, this answer gets all 6 marks. There is a lot of detail. There are almost 2 marks in the first sentence because it says that both use experiments, as the previous answer did, and then adds a bit more. However, it was thought that the two points together were worth 1 mark rather than 2. The point about the number of participants is detailed and so gets 2 marks, and the point about validity is detailed and gets 2 marks.

## Answer 3: Godden and Baddeley with Craik and Tulving

Both Godden and Baddeley and Craik and Tulving use experiment as their research method and use careful controls to aim for cause-and-effect conclusions. ✓✓ They both use a repeated measures design too, which means they both control for participant variables, which is useful when aiming for cause-and-effect conclusions. ✓ Both studies ask their participants to recognise words from a list, which makes them similar, which is not surprising as they both look at cognitive processes. ✓

📝 The first sentence this time gets 2 marks, as it says just a little more than the first sentence of the other two answers — also the idea of cause and effect is returned to later in the answer. There is a third mark for the comparison of the designs. There is a further mark for the point about using word lists. More needed to be said for the other 2 marks. Reliability could have been mentioned, as the use of the controls and research method chosen aims for this. Validity could also have been referred to, as neither study is really valid due to the reliance on word lists, which are unnatural tasks.

**(2) Describe the procedure of Godden and Baddeley (1975).**     (4 marks, AO1)

📝 This question is only about how the study was carried out, so don't give the aim of the study or the results or conclusions. You need to say enough for 4 marks, and a good way of doing this is to say four things about how the study was carried out.

## Answer

The study involved 18 divers who were on a diving holiday in Scotland and agreed to do the study during the holiday, in various locations according to where the dives were planned. ✓ The study used a repeated measures design, as the divers did all four conditions. The conditions were learning the words and recalling them in the same setting and in different settings, with two settings, so there were four conditions. ✓ The divers either learned the words while diving (20 feet deep) or on the shore (sitting with their gear on), and recalled the words either while diving or on the shore. ✓ There were two conditions where learning and recall were in the same setting, and two where there were different settings for learning and recall. It was hard to control the features of the study except for the words and the setting, as the time of day and place of the dive depended on the holiday and what had been arranged, so some features of the situation were not controlled. ✓

📝 There are 4 marks here, and the answer shows that you need to know quite a bit about the studies that you look at in detail. Notice that just saying how many participants there were is not enough for a mark — each mark requires a reasonable amount of information.

**(3) Evaluate one study in cognitive psychology other than Godden and Baddeley (1975). Make sure you identify the study in your answer.** (4 marks, AO2)

*e* This question asks you to give good or bad points about a study. The one covered in this guide is Craik and Tulving, though you may have covered a different one. If you have done a different one, practise answering this question using that study.

## Answer

Craik and Tulving (1975). The study was a laboratory experiment that used different questions to focus on words and then asked for recall/recognition of the words. This is an artificial task and could be said not to be about levels of processing information in general, and so to lack validity. ✓ There was also a lack of ecological validity, in that the study was not in the participants' natural setting, which could have led to results that were not real-life — they might have performed differently rather than as they would in processing in their everyday lives. ✓ The study found that not only was there better recall when semantic processing took place, which was said to be deep processing, but the processing then took longer as well, so it is hard to say whether it is deep processing or length of time processing that leads to the best recall. ✓ As a laboratory experiment, it is replicable because of careful controls such as using a tachistoscope to time how long the words were presented for, so the study can be tested for reliability. ✓

*e* This answer is thorough and you might get more than 1 mark for the points that use terms and explain them clearly as well. However, note that for questions asking you to evaluate in general, you will have to say more to get the mark than for questions that ask for description. Whatever the question, ensure you make your point fully and clearly, as the last two answers illustrate well.

■ ■ ■

# Key issue

**(1) Discuss one key issue you have studied within the cognitive approach, including describing the issue and explaining it with reference to cognitive psychology.** (12 marks, essay)

*e* The marks here are given in levels from an answer that gives no rewardable material (0 marks) to an answer that is well detailed and well focused on the question, giving both description and evaluation. You should describe the issue for a few marks, so that it is clear which issue you are explaining and why it is an issue. Then you should give research — theories and studies — from cognitive psychology to explain the issue. Evaluation can also gain marks and is useful.

## Answer

Eyewitness testimony is an issue that is studied in depth in the cognitive approach, mainly because studies in the approach first highlighted that such testimony might be unreliable. Where someone is convicted of something criminal solely because of eyewitness testimony, there have been many instances of that person being freed on appeal because of understood problems with such testimony. ✓ **AO1** This strongly suggests that there are still people wrongly imprisoned because of eyewitness testimony. It is not suggested that eyewitnesses lie, though that might occur, but that testimony is not as solid as juries and members of the public believe. ✓ **AO1** Elizabeth Loftus carried out many experiments to look at the effect of leading questions on recall, including one study asking about broken glass when there was 'a' broken headlight or 'the' broken headlight. Witnesses seem to take up the suggestion that 'the' broken headlight meant glass, whereas 'a' broken headlight did not suggest glass as strongly. ✓ **AO2** evidence In another study Loftus (with Palmer) showed that changing the verb in a question affected the estimates of the speed of a car in an accident. If cars 'smashed' into one another a witness estimated a higher speed for the car than if cars 'hit' one another. ✓ **AO2** evidence These two studies suggest that the way a witness is questioned will affect their testimony, which shows that eyewitness testimony is not like a tape recording and can be unreliable. ✓ **AO2** evidence summarised Other factors affecting eyewitness testimony, apart from how questions are asked, include how long after the event the witness is questioned and whether the witness is asked in the same context as that in which the incident occurred. ✓ **AO1** Loftus found, however, that eyewitnesses can be swayed, for example, by how questions are asked or what questions are asked, if the information they are recalling is not central to the situation. Where information was central, witnesses were more sure. ✓ **AO1** She carried out experiments, which means they were artificial — for example, when asking about the speed of cars after a car accident she showed participants a film. In a real-life accident a witness would be more emotional and that might affect their memory — so her study was not valid. ✓ **AO2** Also, when eyewitness testimony is being studied, the situations that a participant is put into, such as thinking about car accidents, can be stressful, and ethical guidelines suggest that participants are not supposed to be distressed. ✓ **AO2**

🖉 This answer is not marked point by point, but where a relevant point is made, there is a tick to help you to see how to make relevant points. There is a balance of AO1 and AO2 marks, which is good in this sort of essay, and there is good use of terminology, with clear communication. Giving details about some of the cases where eyewitness testimony has led to a conviction that has subsequently been quashed because of over-reliance on eyewitness testimony would be useful, to add depth to the essay. This essay is likely to be in the band just below the top band, though with a bit more detail it would be a top-band essay. You would expect to get around 9 of the 12 marks for this essay.

■ ■ ■

# Practical

Within cognitive psychology you will have carried out an experiment on some aspect of either memory or forgetting.

**(1) (a) Give the aim of your study.** (1 mark, AO3)

> *e* The study on which we focus here for answers is a version of the Craik and Tulving study. You should answer this section using the practical you did for your own course.

## Answer

The aim was to see if semantic processing led to the best recall compared to structural or phonemic processing. ✓

> *e* This is fine and clear.

**(b) Explain one control that you put into place, other than sampling or standardised instructions.** (2 marks, AO3)

> *e* There are situational and participant variables that need to be controlled in an experiment, and the four studies in your course in cognitive psychology are experiments. Sampling and standardised instructions control participant variables, so consider another participant variable or a situational variable for your own study.

## Answer 1

The situation was controlled.

> *e* This is not enough for a mark, as you must be specific.

## Answer 2

One control is that the questions used to gather the data are the same for everyone, including being typed the same, ✓ using the same word lists for recognition and asking the same questions. ✓

> *e* This is fine for the 2 marks, as making the apparatus the same is a necessary control and enough is said for 2 marks.

**(c) Explain how you gave (or could have given) your participants the right to withdraw.** (3 marks, AO3)

> *e* There are 3 marks for explaining how the right to withdraw was given. This means that good detail is required.

## Answer

Standardised instructions were read out to participants just before they started to complete the questionnaire, which had the list of questions to gather the data. The instructions thanked everyone in advance for their cooperation and informed them clearly that, at that point, they could withdraw from the study. ✓ The instructions went on to say that each participant could withdraw from the study at any time and would be able to withdraw their data at the end if they wished to. ✓ At the end of the study the participants were thanked again and asked again if their data could be used, and they were reminded that they could withdraw their data if they wished. ✓ Nobody did and all seemed happy to have taken part.

*e* This gets the full 3 marks because there is quite a bit of depth. Note that you have to make your points clearly to get the marks.

**(d) What was the independent variable and how did you operationalise it?**                                                                                  (4 marks, AO3)

*e* The IV is usually fully operationalised but you could give a general IV for this answer first, as you then have to show how it is operationalised anyway. The IV might not get a mark until it is operationalised when given as an answer to another question, but as there are 4 marks here for the IV, detail is needed.

## Answer

The IV was whether structural, phonemic or semantic processing was taking place, ✓ and this was operationalised based largely on Craik and Tulving. Structural processing involved answering whether a word was in capital letters or lower case. ✓ Phonemic processing involved answering whether a word rhymed with another word or not. ✓ Semantic processing involved answering whether a word fitted into a particular sentence or not. ✓

*e* This answer gets all 4 marks, but Craik and Tulving is useful for this sort of question as there are three conditions. Where there is only one condition it will be harder to get full marks for this question. You could justify why the operationalising had taken place.